Riddles of the Soul

by Rudolf Steiner

MERCURY PRESS

This edition of *Riddles of the Soul* is a translation
of *Von Seelenrätzeln*, GA Nr: 21
by William Lindeman.
The translation was made from
the 5th German edition published by
Verlag der Rudolf Steiner Nachlassverwaltung,
Dornach, Switzerland 1983.

ISBN 978-1-957569-48-2

MERCURY PRESS
an imprint of SteinerBooks
834 Main Street, PO Box 358
Spencertown, New York 12165
www.steinerbooks.org

CONTENTS

Introduction

If ever a difficult book was worth every minute of effort it requires, this is it—all of it, not just the parts already published as *The Case For Anthroposophy*.

Rudolf Steiner's own words, spoken in Dornach on February 4, 1923 shortly after the burning of the first Goetheanum, set the tone:

> In the first essay of my book *Riddles of the Soul*, I reiterate that a person bound to contemporary civilization believes that we confront all kinds of insurmountable limits to our ability to know. Such a person feels relief at this. His relief, however, only indicates a desire not to wake up. He wants to remain asleep. But anyone who in a modern sense wants to enter the spiritual world must begin to grapple with inner soul tasks at precisely the spot where the other person sets limits to knowledge. And as he begins to grapple with the ideas arising at this borderland, there opens up for him gradually, in stages, a view of the spiritual world. One must in fact take what anthroposophy offers in the way it is meant.
>
> Take this first essay of *Riddles of the Soul*. Its content may be imperfectly expressed, but one can certainly discover in it the intention with which it was written! Its purpose is to awaken the realization: If I stop where modern civilization stops, then the world is actually boarded up for me. From natural science I try to go further. There come the barriers. There the world is boarded up for me.
>
> The content of this first essay of *Riddles of the Soul* is an effort to knock away those boards with spades.

When we feel that we are working with spades to knock away the planks that have boarded up the world for centuries, when we consider the words to be spades, then we arrive at the soul-spiritual realm.

Most people have the unconscious feeling that an essay like the first one in *Riddles of the Soul* is written with a pen from which ink flows. But it is not written with a pen. It is written with soul spades, which want to rip away the planks that board up the world, i.e., which want to clear away the limitations of natural science, but want to do so with inner work of the soul. The reader must participate in this activation of the soul, however, when reading an essay such as this.

In addendum 6 on page 131 of this book, Rudolf Steiner describes for the first time his thirty-year-long work in relating the three soul forces of thinking, feeling, and willing to the three systems of the body: the nervous, rhythmical, and metabolic. In the same section we are shown why he believed the theoretical division into sensory and motor nerves to be so harmful.

The essay on Max Dessoir challenges us to experience the subtlety and exactitude required of a spiritually striving modern person. As Rudolf Steiner states on page 54, "the thorough permeating of concepts with consciousness is necessary if these concepts are to have a relation to the genuine spiritual world."

W. L.

Preface

The essays collected in this book were written by me in order to present something of what I believe I must say as validation of the anthroposophical path of knowledge.

In the first essay on anthropology and anthroposophy ("Where Natural Science and Spiritual Science Meet"), I seek to show briefly that the true natural-scientific approach not only does not stand in any contradiction to what I understand by "anthroposophy," but that anthroposophy's spiritual-scientific path must even be demanded as something essential by anthropology's means of knowledge. There must be an anthroposophical spiritual science if the anthropological knowledge of natural science wishes to be what it must claim to be. Either the reasons for the existence of an anthroposophy are legitimate, or true validity cannot be attributed to natural-scientific insights either. This is what I endeavor to present in the first essay in a form not yet expressly stated in the books I have already published, although present there in a germinal state.

Concerning the second essay, "Max Dessoir on Anthroposophy," I must admit that I had no subjective desire to write it. Yet it had to be written, because had I not done so, the misconception could have arisen in many circles that the adherent of anthroposophy shrinks from entering into a scientific discussion with adherents of other ways of picturing things. To be sure, I leave many attacks on anthroposophy entirely unanswered, not only because I do not consider polemics in this area to be my task, but because the great majority of these attacks lack the seriousness necessary for a fruitful discussion in this area. Even those assailants who believe they should combat anthroposophy for scientific reasons often do not know at all how unscientific their objections are compared to the scientific thinking that anthroposophy considers necessary for itself.

I deeply regret that the essay on Max Dessoir's attack on anthroposophy could not be what I gladly would have made it. I would have liked to enter into a discussion of the way of picturing things advocated by Dessoir on the one hand and by anthroposophy on the other. Instead of this I am obliged by Dessoir's "critique" to show that he presents his readers with a distorted picture of my views, and then speaks, not about them, but about what he has made of them, which has nothing at all to do with my views. I had to show how Max Dessoir "reads" the books that he undertakes to attack. Therefore my essay is filled with discussion of things that might seem trivial. How can one proceed differently, however, when trivial details are needed for presenting the truth? I leave it up to the readers of my book—who can decide from it how much this "critic" could understand of my views with his way of reading my books [*]—to judge whether Max Dessoir has the right to debase the anthroposophy advocated by me through his act of including it in spiritual streams of which he says that they are "a mixture of incorrect interpretations of certain soul processes and incorrectly judged relics of a vanished world view."

I must say just the opposite about the third essay, "Franz Brentano, in Memoriam." Writing it was my deepest need.

---

[*] With respect to other hostile books and articles, please see the "Closing Remark" on page 154 of this book. Basically I do not feel it suitable to the seriousness of the present time to publish a polemic like the one *necessitated* for me by Dessoir's book. It is only that in this case I *could* not avoid an answer to the provocation of *such* an attack.

4

And if I regret anything about it, it is that I did not write it long ago and could not make the attempt to bring it to Brentano's attention while he still lived. It is only that, although I have been an ardent reader of Brentano's writings for a long time, his life's work has only now appeared before my soul in such a way that I can present its relation to anthroposophy as is done in this book. The passing of this revered man moved me to relive in thought his life work; and only from this did my views of his life work reach the provisional conclusions that underlie the discussions in my essay.

I have added on to these three essays "Sketches of Some of the Ramifications of the Content of This Book," which represent the findings of anthroposophical research. Present-day circumstances dictate that in these presentations I give indications of findings that actually necessitate a much fuller discussion, like that given in my lectures, although there too in an incomplete fashion still. In these presentations I establish some of the scientific connections that must be drawn between anthroposophy and philosophy, psychology, and physiology.

It might very well seem as though at the present time the interests of human beings must go in a different direction than the following discussions are moving. Nevertheless, I believe that such discussions do not draw us away from the serious duties of the immediate present; on the contrary, what lies in these discussions serves precisely this present day through impulses that have less directly striking but therefore all the stronger connections to our experience of this present day.

Berlin, September 10, 1917   Rudolf Steiner

I

Where Natural Science and Spiritual Science Meet

Max Dessoir's book *Beyond the Soul* (*Vom Jenseits der Seele*) contains a brief section in which the anthroposophically oriented spiritual science advocated by me is portrayed as scientifically invalid. Now it might seem to many that a discussion with people who take Dessoir's point of view about science must prove altogether unfruitful to anyone advocating spiritual-scientific anthroposophy. For, such an advocate asserts the existence of a purely spiritual region of experience that a Dessoir fundamentally rejects and consigns to the realm of fantasy. Discussion of the findings of spiritual-scientific knowledge, therefore, might only seem possible with someone who already has reason to believe that such a spiritual-scientific region exists.

This view would be correct if the advocate of anthroposophy presented nothing more than his own inner personal experiences and simply placed them beside the results of the science based on sensory observation and the scientific processing of such observations. Then one could say: the adherent of natural science refuses in fact to regard the experiences of the spiritual researcher as realities; the researcher in the spiritual realm can only make an impression with his findings on those who have already adopted his own point of view.

This opinion, however, rests upon a misunderstanding of what I mean by anthroposophy. It is true that this anthroposophy is founded upon soul experiences that are attained

6

independently of sense impressions and independently of scientific judgments based only upon sense impressions. Therefore the two kinds of experiences, sensory and extrasensory, seem at first to be separated by an unbridgeable chasm.

But this is not so. There is a common ground where both approaches must meet, and where discussion is possible. This common ground can be described in the following way.

Out of experiences that are not just personal to him, the advocate of anthroposophy believes himself justified in stating that human activity in knowledge can be developed further from the point at which those researchers stop who want to base themselves only upon sensory observation and intellectual judgment of such observation.

To avoid continuous, long-winded paraphrases, I would like to use the word "anthropology" from now on to designate that approach in science which bases itself on sensory observation and the intellectual processing of such observation, asking the reader to permit me this uncommon usage. In what follows, "anthropology" means only what I have just described. In this sense, anthroposophy believes itself able to begin its research where anthropology leaves off.[*]

The advocate of anthropology limits himself to relating his intellectual concepts—experienced in the soul—to his

---

[*] Although the anthroposophy advocated by me stands on a completely different ground, with its results, than the presentations of Robert Zimmermann in his book *Anthroposophy* (1881), still I believe myself justified in using the concept by which he characterized the difference between anthroposophy and anthropology. As the content of his anthroposophy, however, Zimmermann only draws together into an abstract schema the concepts provided by anthropology. For him, the knowing vision that is the basis for what I mean by anthroposophy lies outside the domain of scientific procedure. His anthroposophy differs from anthropology only through the fact that the former first submits the concepts it receives from the latter to a process like that of Herbart's philosophy, before making these concepts into the content of its purely intellectual schema of ideas.

sense perceptions. The advocate of anthroposophy observes that these concepts—apart from the fact that we relate them to sense impressions—are able in addition to unfold a life of their own within the soul. And that, by unfolding this life within the soul, these concepts effect a development of the soul itself. The advocate of anthroposophy sees how the soul, if it is sufficiently attentive to this development, discovers spiritual organs within its own being. (In using this expression "spiritual organs," I am adopting and extending the linguistic usage of Goethe when he speaks in his world view of "spiritual eyes" and "spiritual ears.")[*] Such spiritual organs, therefore, are for the soul what sense organs are for the body. These spiritual organs must of course be understood as being *entirely* of a soul nature. Any attempt to connect them with one or another bodily configuration must be strictly rejected by anthroposophy. Anthroposophy must not picture these spiritual organs as extending in any way beyond the soul realm or encroaching upon the structure of the body. It would regard any such encroachment as a pathological configuration, to be strictly excluded from its domain. The way anthroposophy portrays the development of our spiritual organs should be strong enough proof—to anyone who really informs himself about it—that the researcher in the real spiritual realm arrives at the same conclusions as anthropologists about abnormal soul experiences like illusions, visions, and hallucinations.[**] Any

---

[*] A more detailed presentation and justification of this notion of "spiritual organs" can be found in my book *The Riddle of Man*, Mercury Press, 1990, page 125ff. and in my books on Goethe's world view.

[**] The inner experiences that the soul must undergo in gaining the use of its spiritual organs are described in a number of my books, but especially in *Knowledge of the Higher Worlds and Its Attainment* and in the second part of *Occult Science, an Outline*.

confusion of anthroposophical findings with abnormal, so-called soul experiences rests entirely upon misunderstanding or insufficient knowledge of what anthroposophy actually maintains. And anyone who studies and understands anthroposophy's description of the path to development of our spiritual organs will certainly not fall prey to the notion that this path could lead to pathological configurations or states. The insightful person, in fact, will recognize that every stage of soul experience that a human being passes through on the anthroposophical path to spiritual perception lies in a realm that is entirely of a soul nature; alongside this realm, our sensory experience and normal intellectual activity will continue, unaltered, as they were before this soul realm opened up for us. The great number of misunderstandings holding sway in precisely this area of anthroposophical knowledge stems from the fact that it is difficult for many to bring something of a purely soul nature into the sphere of their attention. The power to picture mentally[*] fails such people the moment this ability is not supported by the sight of something sense-perceptible. Their power to picture mentally is then dampened down, even below the level of dreams, into dreamless sleep, where it is no longer conscious. One could say that such people, in their consciousness, are filled with the aftereffects or the direct effects of sense impressions, and that, alongside this fullness, a sleep is occurring that blocks out what would be

---

[*] *Sich Vorstellen* means to visualize, to picture to oneself mentally. The ability to "place something before oneself inwardly" is a crucial factor in spiritual development and as such is referred to constantly in this essay. How do we hold something up before our inner eye? What is the attention we focus upon it? Who does this? What is the nature of mental pictures (*Vorstellungen*) themselves? Such questions are among the many painful riddles that ordinary consciousness cannot solve, and that bring us up against an invisible world. Translator.

recognized as being of a soul nature if it could be grasped. One could even say that the essential nature of soul phenomena is subject to such profound misunderstanding by many people just because they cannot wake up to the soul element as they can to the sense-perceptible content of consciousness.

The fact that there are people in this situation whose degree of attention is only at the level produced by ordinary external life need not surprise anyone who can grasp the point, for example, of a reproach which Franz Brentano made to William James on this subject.

Brentano writes that one must "differentiate between our activity of perceiving and its object, i.e., between perceiving and what is perceived" ("and these two differ from each other as certainly as my present memory differs from the past event I am remembering; or, to make an even more drastic comparison: they differ as much as my hatred of an enemy differs from the object of this hatred"), and Brentano adds that one sees this error cropping up here and there. He continues:

William James, among others, embraced this error and went to some length to validate it at the International Congress on Psychology (Rome, 1905). Because, according to James, when I look out into a room, my vision appears along with the room; and, furthermore, because my mental images of sense-perceptible objects differ only in strength from the visual images directly stimulated by these objects; and, finally, because we call some objects beautiful, yet the difference between beautiful and ugly is connected to differences in emotions: therefore, soul and physical phenomena should no longer be regarded as two different classes of phenomena!

I find it hard to understand how the speaker himself could not feel the weakness of these arguments. To appear at the same time does not mean to appear as the same thing; just as existing at the same time does not mean existing as the same thing. Descartes could therefore recommend without self-contradiction that one deny—at least initially—the existence of the room I see, and regard as indubitable only the existence of my *vision* of the room. But if James' first argument is invalid, then obviously the second is also; for, what does it matter whether imagining differs from seeing only in degree of intensity, since, according to James, even if the degree of intensity were the same in both, the total congruency of imagining with seeing would still only represent congruency with a soul phenomenon? In his third argument, James speaks of beauty.... It is certainly a strange logic that could conclude—from the fact that pleasure in the beautiful is of a soul nature—that the object with whose appearance the pleasure is connected must also be of a soul nature. If that were so, then every dislike would be identical with what one dislikes, and one would have to be careful not to regret a past mistake, since, along with this remorse, the mistake, being identical with the remorse, would repeat itself.

With arguments like these, however, we need not fear that his authority—to which, among German psychologists, there is unfortunately added that of Mach—will cause many to fail to recognize the most obvious differences.

---

* See F. Brentano, *Research into a Psychology of the Senses*, Leipzig, 1907, p. 96f.

Actually, this "failure to recognize the most obvious differences" is no rare occurrence. It is based on the fact that our power of mental picturing can unfold the necessary attentiveness only for sense impressions, whereas the actual soul activity that is also occurring is present to consciousness as little as what is experienced in a state of sleep. We are dealing here with two streams of experience; one of these is apprehended in a waking state; the other—the soul stream—is grasped simultaneously, but only with an attentiveness as weak as the mental perception we have in sleep, i.e., it is hardly grasped at all. We must by no means ignore the fact that during our ordinary waking state, the soul disposition of sleep does not simply cease, but continues to exist alongside our waking experience, and that the actual soul element enters the realm of perception only when the human being awakens not only to the sense world—as this occurs in ordinary consciousness—but awakens also to a soul existence, as is the case in *seeing consciousness*. It hardly matters now whether this soul element is denied—in a crudely materialistic sense—by the condition of sleep (to the soul element) that accompanies our waking state, or whether, because unseen, the soul element is confused with the physical, as in James' case; the results are nearly the same: both lead to fatal nearsightedness. But it is not surprising that the soul element so often remains unperceivable, if even a philosopher like William James is unable to differentiate it correctly from the physical.

---

* The awakening of those soul faculties which, in ordinary consciousness, are unawakened is described in more detail in my book *The Riddle of Man*, page 132ff.

With people as little able as William James to distinguish between the actual soul element and the content of what the soul experiences through the senses, it is difficult to discuss that region of our soul's being in which the development of spiritual organs is to be observed. For, this development occurs precisely where his attention is unable to direct itself. This development leads from an intellectual knowing to a knowing that sees.*

But now, through the ability to perceive the actual soul element, we have as yet fulfilled only the very first precondition, which makes it possible to direct our spiritual gaze to where anthroposophy seeks the development of soul organs. For, what meets this gaze at first compares to anthroposophy's description of a soul-being equipped with spiritual organs the way an undifferentiated living cell compares to an organism endowed with sense organs. The soul becomes conscious of possessing the individual spiritual organs themselves, however, only to the extent that it is able to use these organs. For, these organs are not something at rest; they are in continuous movement. And when they are not in use, one also cannot be conscious of their presence. For them, therefore, perceiving and being used are synonymous. In my anthroposophical writings, I describe how the development—and along with it the perceptibility—of these organs comes to light. I will indicate here only a little of what can be said in this regard.

Anyone who devotes himself to reflection on the experiences caused by sense-perceptible phenomena encounters questions everywhere that this reflection seems unable to

---

* For a more extensive validation of what is stated here, please see addendum 1 on page 107: "The Philosophical Validation of Anthroposophy."

answer at first. The pursuit of such reflections leads the adherents of anthropology to set certain limits to knowledge. One need only remember how Du Bois-Reymond, in his discourse on the limits of natural science, states that one cannot know the essential nature of matter or of the simplest phenomenon of consciousness. Now one can stop short at such points in one's reflections and surrender to the opinion: there human knowledge is in fact confronted by insurmountable barriers. And one can resign oneself to the fact that knowledge is attainable only on this side of the barrier, and that beyond this only inklings, feelings, hopes, and wishes are possible, with which "science" could have nothing to do.

Or else one can start at such points to form hypotheses about a region transcending the sense-perceptible world. In this case one employs the intellect, believing that it is justified in extending its judgments out over a region of which the senses perceive nothing. In such an undertaking, one runs the risk that nonbelievers will declare that the intellect has no right to judge a reality for which it lacks the foundations of sense perceptions. For only sense perceptions could provide a content for the intellect's judgment. Without such content, its concepts must remain empty.

Anthroposophically oriented spiritual science does not relate to "limits of knowledge" in either of these two ways. It does not form hypotheses about the supersensible world because it must agree with those who feel that any basis for reflection is lost if mental pictures are left in the same form as when taken from sense perceptions, and yet are to be applied in a realm transcending the sense world.

Anthroposophy does not relate to "limits of knowledge" in the first way either, because it realizes that in our encounter with these so-called limits of knowledge, some-thing can be experienced by the soul that has nothing to do with the content of mental pictures gained from sense per-ception. If the soul focuses only upon this latter content, then, if its self-examination is honest, it must admit that this content can reveal nothing directly to our activity of know-ing except a copy of what we experience through the senses. The situation changes if the soul goes further and asks itself: What can be experienced within the soul itself when it fills itself with those mental pictures to which it is led when confronted by our usual limits of knowledge? After suffi-cient self-examination, the soul can then say to itself: Through such mental pictures I cannot, in the ordinary sense of the word, know anything; but in the event that I really make *this* powerlessness of my knowing activity in-wardly visible to myself, then I become aware how these mental pictures work within my own self. As ordinary cog-nitive pictures, these mental pictures remain mute; but the more their muteness communicates itself to our conscious-ness, the more these mental pictures take on an inner life of their own that unites with the life of the soul. And the soul then notices how, with this experience, it is in a situation comparable to that of a blind being who has also not experi-enced much development of its sense of touch. Such a being would at first keep bumping into things. It would feel the resistance of outer reality. And from this generalized sensa-tion, it could develop an inner life for itself, filled with a primitive consciousness that no longer has merely the gen-eral sensation of bumping into things, but that differentiates this sensation and distinguishes between hardness and soft-ness, smoothness and roughness, etc.

In the same way, the soul can hold and differentiate its experience of the mental pictures it forms in its encounter with the limits of knowledge. The soul learns to experience that these limits represent nothing more than what arises when the soul is touched by the spiritual world in a soul way. The dawning awareness of such limits becomes an experience for the soul that can be compared with the experience of touch in the sense world.* What the soul formerly regarded as limits to knowledge it now sees as a soul-spiritual touching by a spiritual world. And out of the soul's attentiveness to its experiences with the various pictures it makes for itself at this borderland, the general sensing of a spiritual world differentiates for the soul into diverse perceptions of a spiritual world. In this way, the spiritual world's lowest form of perceptibility, so to speak, becomes an experience. This characterizes merely the very first opening of the soul to the spiritual world. But it also shows that the spiritual experiences striven for in what I mean by anthroposophy do not point in the direction of general, nebulous, emotional experiences that the soul has of itself, but rather in the direction of something that can be developed in a lawful way into a true inner experience. This is not the place to show how this first primitive spiritual perception can be intensified by further soul practices in such a way that one can speak of other, in a certain way, higher kinds of perception besides this soul-spiritual blind groping. For a description of such soul practices I must refer the reader to my anthroposophical books and essays. Here only the basic

* Limits to knowledge like those discussed above do not merely present themselves in the small number of which most people are aware; they occur in great number along the paths that intelligent reflection, according to its own inner nature, must take in order to gain a relation to true reality. Please see addendum 2 on page 114: "The Appearance of Limits to Knowledge."

principle of spiritual perception was to be indicated of which anthroposophy speaks.

I would like, through a comparison, to clarify still further how the whole attitude of soul in anthroposophical spiritual investigation differs from that of anthropology. Picture to yourself a number of wheat kernels. These can be used as food. But one can also plant them in the earth so that other wheat plants can grow from them. Likewise, one can hold mental pictures—gained through sense impressions—within one's consciousness in such a way as to experience them as copies of sense-perceptible reality. Or, one can experience these mental pictures in such a way as to let work in the soul the power these pictures exercise through what they are, irrespective of the fact that they reproduce sense perceptions. The first way that mental pictures were described as working in the soul can be compared with what becomes of wheat kernels when they are taken up as food by a living being; the second way, with the production of a new wheat plant from each kernel.

This comparison, to be sure, is only meant to focus on the fact that from the seed there arises a plant similar to its progenitors; and that from a mental picture working in the soul there arises within the soul a power that is effective in developing spiritual organs. And one must also consider the fact that our first awareness of such inner powers can only be kindled by mental pictures that work as forcefully as those mental pictures we described as occurring at the borderland of knowledge; once awakened, however, this awareness of such powers can find other mental pictures that can also be effective—to a lesser degree, it is true—in helping one progress upon this path.

At the same time, this comparison points to a result of anthroposophical investigation into the essential nature of our life in mental pictures. Just as a seed, when it is processed into food, is lifted out of the course of development that lies within its own primal being and that leads to the formation of a new plant, so a mental picture too is diverted from its own essential course of development when it is used by the picturing soul to reproduce a sense perception. The development particular to a mental picture through its own essential nature is to work as a power in the development of the soul. Just as little as one discovers the plant's laws of development when one investigates the nutritive value of its seeds, can one discover the essential nature of mental pictures when one investigates the way mental picturing brings forth a cognitive reproduction of the sense-perceptible reality it communicates. This does not mean to say that such an investigation cannot be undertaken. This is just as possible as investigating the nutritive value of seeds. But just as a study of the nutritive value of seeds addresses something different than the developmental laws of plant growth, so an epistemology that investigates how the cognitive power of mental pictures reproduces reality informs us about something different than the essential nature of our life of mental picturing. Just as little as it lies prefigured in the essential nature of a seed to become food, does it lie in the essential nature of mental picturing to provide cognitive reproductions of reality. Yes, we can even say that it is as completely external to the seed's own nature to use it as food as it is to the actual nature of mental pictures to use them to reproduce reality in cognition. The truth is that in its mental pictures the soul grasps its own evolving being. And only through the soul's own activity does it occur that mental pictures become the mediators of any knowledge of reality.[*]

Now, as to how mental pictures become mediators of such knowledge, anthroposophical observation, which employs spiritual organs, arrives at different conclusions than those epistemologists do who reject this observation. Anthroposophical observation reveals the following.

Mental pictures, as they are in their own primal nature, do in fact form a part of the life of the soul; but they cannot become conscious in the soul as long as the soul does not consciously employ its spiritual organs. As long as these mental pictures are active in a way corresponding to their own essential nature, they remain unconscious in the soul. The soul *lives* by virtue of them, but can *know* nothing of them. These mental pictures must dampen down their own life in order to become conscious soul experiences for ordinary consciousness. This dampening down occurs with every sense perception. Thus, when the soul receives a sense impression, there occurs a laming of our life in mental pictures; and the soul experiences this lamed mental picturing consciously as the mediator of our knowledge of external reality.[**] All mental pictures that the soul relates to an outer sense-perceptible reality are inner spiritual experiences whose *life* has been dampened down. Everything that one thinks regarding the outer sense world consists of deadened mental pictures. Now it is not as though the life of mental pictures were lost, however; it leads its existence, separated from the realm of con-

---

[*] A more detailed case is made for these views in the last chapter of my book *The Riddles of Philosophy*: "Sketch of a Perspective of an Anthroposophy."

[**] Please see addendum 3 on page 118: "The Abstractness of Our Concepts."

sciousness, in the unconscious spheres of the soul. And there it is to be found again by our spiritual organs. Now, just as the deadened mental pictures can be related by the soul to the sense world, so the living mental pictures grasped by our spiritual organs can be related to the spiritual world.

The mental pictures described above as occurring to us at the borderland of knowledge are those that, by their very nature, do not let themselves be lamed; therefore, they resist any relation to sense-perceptible reality. Precisely through this fact, they become the points of departure for spiritual perception.

In my anthroposophical books, I have called the mental pictures that are grasped as living ones by the soul "Imaginative mental pictures." One misunderstands what is meant here by "Imaginative," if one confuses it with the pictorial *form* of expression that must be used to point to such mental pictures in a suitable way. What is actually meant by "Imaginative" can be clarified in the following way. When someone has a sense perception, while the outer object is making an impression on him, the perception has a certain inner strength for him. When he turns away from the object, he can then only represent it to himself in an inner picture. But this mental picture has little inner strength. It is shadowy, so to speak, when compared with the mental picture that occurs while the outer object is present. If a person wants to enliven the mental pictures that are present in his soul in the shadowy form characteristic of ordinary consciousness, he saturates them with the aftereffects of sense perception. He makes the mental picture into an *image* he can observe [inwardly]. Such images are certainly nothing other than the results of interaction between mental picturing and sense perception. The "Imaginative" mental pictures of anthroposophy do not arise at all in this way. In order to bring them forth, the soul must know this inner process of uniting the life of mental pictures with sense impressions so exactly that it can prevent any sense impressions—or their aftereffects, as the case may be—from flowing into its life of mental picturing. One can achieve this exclusion of perception's aftereffects only if one has learned to know how mental picturing is gripped by these aftereffects. Only then is one in a position to unite the spiritual organs in a living way with the essential being of mental picturing and thereby receive impressions from spiritual reality. Through this, the life of mental pictures is permeated from an entirely different quarter than in sense perception. One's experiences are essentially different from those to be had from sense perceptions. And yet it is possible to describe these experiences. This can be done in the following way.

When the human being perceives the color yellow he does not merely have a visual experience in his soul; a nuance of feeling accompanies what the soul experiences. This feeling may vary in strength from person to person, but it will never be totally absent. In the beautiful chapter of his *Color Theory* on the sensory-ethical effects of colors, Goethe describes in a quite vivid manner the participation of our feeling in red, yellow, green, etc. Now when the soul perceives something in a particular region of the spirit, it can happen that this spiritual perception is accompanied in the soul by the same nuance of feeling as occurs in the sense perception of yellow. One knows then that one is having a particular spiritual experience. In this mental picture, of course, one does not confront what one confronts in a sense perception of a yellow color. Yet, as a nuance of feeling, one has the same inner experience as when the eye is confronted by a yellow color. One says then: I perceive the spiritual experience as "yellow." In order to express oneself even more exactly, one could perhaps say: I perceive something that is like "yellow" for my soul. But this description is unnecessary for anyone who has learned from anthroposophical literature how the process leading to spiritual perception occurs. This literature points clearly enough to the fact that the reality accessible to spiritual perception does not confront the spiritual organs like a rarefied sense-perceptible object or process, or in such a way that it could be reproduced through mental pictures that are perceptible in the ordinary way.[*]

* * *

Just as the soul, through its spiritual organs, learns to know the spiritual world lying outside of the human being, so it also learns to know the spiritual being of man himself. Anthroposophy regards this spiritual being as a member of the spiritual world. Anthroposophy proceeds from observation of one part of the spiritual world to mental pictures about the human being of what reveals itself in the human body as a spiritual human being. Working from the opposite direction, anthropology also arrives at mental pictures about the human being. When anthroposophy develops the kinds of observations described in this essay, it arrives at views about the spiritual being of man that manifests in the sense

---

[*] For further clarification of what has just been expressed, please see addendum 4 on page 123: "An Important Characteristic of Spiritual Perception."

world through its body. The flower of this manifestation is human consciousness, which allows sense impressions to live on in the form of mental pictures. By proceeding from experiences of the spiritual world outside man to man himself, anthroposophy ultimately finds the human being living in a sense-perceptible body and, in this body, elaborating his consciousness of sense-perceptible reality. The last thing anthroposophy, on its path, discovers about the human being is the soul's living activity in mental pictures, which anthroposophy is able to express in coherent imaginative pictures. Then, at the end of its path of spiritual investigation, so to speak, anthroposophy can employ its vision further and see how the real life of mental pictures is lamed by the perceiving senses. With the light it sheds from the spiritual quarter, anthroposophy shows this lamed life of mental pictures to be characteristic of man's life in the sense world, insofar as he forms mental pictures. In this way, as one of the last results of its investigations, anthroposophy arrives at a philosophy of the human being. What lies on its path down to this point is to be found purely in a spiritual realm. With the results of what it has found on its spiritual path, anthroposophy arrives at a characterization of the human being who lives in the sense world.

Anthropology investigates the realms of the sense world. Proceeding on its way, it also arrives at the human being. He presents himself to anthropology as drawing together the facts of the sense world in his bodily organization in such a way that from this drawing together a consciousness arises through which outer reality is presented in mental pictures. The anthropologist sees mental pictures arising from the human organism. In observing this, he must come to a halt in a certain sense. With mere anthropology, he cannot apprehend the inner, lawful connectedness of mental pictures. Just as anthroposophy, at the end of its path through spiritual experiences, still looks at the spiritual being of man—insofar as this manifests through the perceptions of the senses—so anthropology, at the end of its path through the sense world, must look at the way the sense-perceptible human being is active in mental picturing in its encounter with sense perceptions. And when it observes this, anthropology finds that this activity is not sustained by the organic laws of the body, but by the thought-laws of logic. But logic is not a region that can be entered in the same way as the other regions of anthropology. In thinking that is governed by logic, laws hold sway that can no longer be regarded as those of the bodily organization. As the human being works with these laws, the same logical activity reveals itself in him that anthroposophy encounters at the end of its path. It is just that the anthropologist sees this logical activity in the light shed from the sense-perceptible realm. He sees the lamed mental pictures and, by acknowledging the existence of logic, he also concedes that in these mental pictures laws are operative from a world that is indeed united with the sense world, but does not coincide with it. In man's life of mental pictures, which is carried by a logical activity, there manifests to the anthropologist the sense-perceptible human being who extends into the spiritual world. In this way, as the final results of its investigations, anthropology arrives at a philosophy about the human being. What lies on its path up to this point lies purely in the sense world.[*]

_____

[*] Like the thoughts on page 13, what has been indicated here can be clarified further in a certain direction by addendum 1 on page 107: "The Philosophical Validation of Anthroposophy."

If these two paths—the anthroposophical and the anthropological—are followed in the right way, they meet at the same point. Anthroposophy brings with it to this meeting a picture of the living spiritual human being and shows how he develops, in sense-perceptible existence, the consciousness that is present between birth and death while the life of supersensible consciousness is lamed. Anthropology, at this meeting point, shows a picture of the sense-perceptible human being who apprehends himself in consciousness, but who extends up into spiritual existence and lives in that essential beingness which reaches beyond birth and death. At this meeting point, a really fruitful understanding is possible between anthroposophy and anthropology. This understanding will occur if both progress to a philosophy of the human being. The philosophy of the human being that emerges from anthroposophy will in fact produce a picture of him painted in an entirely different medium than that provided by an anthropological philosophy of the human being; but those who look at both pictures will be able to find a harmony between their mental pictures similar to that between the negative of a photograph and the corresponding positive print.

This essay, I hope, has shown how the question raised at the beginning—about the possibility of a fruitful discussion between anthropology and anthroposophy—can be answered in the affirmative, especially from the anthroposophical point of view.

II

Max Dessoir on Anthroposophy

The preceding essay shows how strongly and concretely the anthroposophist (spiritual scientist) can wish to come to terms with the anthropologist (natural scientist). One might think that a book with purposes like those of Max Dessoir would lend itself to just such a discussion. From the anthroposophical viewpoint, Dessoir's book is written in the anthropological mode. It bases itself upon the findings of sense observation; and wants to employ the kind of thinking and research usual to the natural-scientific approach. His book belongs to what we mean by anthropological science.

In that part of his book entitled "Anthroposophy," Max Dessoir wants to deliver a critique of the anthroposophical views presented in my books.* He tries to reproduce in his own way some of the material from these books and then adds his critical comments. This could show us, therefore, what each of the two realms of thought has to say about one or another aspect of human striving for knowledge.

Let me now present and discuss what Max Dessoir writes.

Dessoir wishes to point to my support of the view that the human soul, through inner development, can attain the ability to use its spiritual organs, and through this can bring itself into the same kind of connection with the spiritual world that it has to the sense world through its physical sense organs. You can see from my first essay how I picture

---

* Pages 254-263 of his book, *Vom Jenseits der Seele, die Geheimwissenschaften in kritischer Betrachtung; Beyond the Soul, A Critical View of the Arcane Sciences*, by Max Dessoir, Ferdinand Enke Press, Stuttgart, 1917.

what must occur in the soul in order for it to arrive at perception of the spiritual life. Max Dessoir presents in his way what I have said about this in my books. He writes:

Through this kind of inner work, the soul attains what all philosophy has sought. To be sure, we must be careful not to confuse the body-free consciousness with dream-like clairvoyance or hypnotic processes. When our soul powers are enhanced, the "I" can experience itself above consciousness, in a kind of densification and individualization of the spirit, as it were; yes, the "I," in its perception of colors and sounds, can even exclude the mediation of the body from this experience.

Dessoir then inserts the following footnote: "Refuting these assertions individually is not worth the while." So, Dessoir adds to my views about spiritual perception that I assert that in perceiving colors and sounds one can exclude the mediation of the body. Please look back at what I said in the preceding essay about the experiences of the soul through its spiritual organs, and how the soul arrives at expression of these experiences in color and sound pictures. You will see that, from the point of view of anthroposophy, I could not assert anything more absurd than that the soul, "in its perception of colors and sounds, can exclude the mediation of the body." If I ever did make such a claim, it *would* then be correct to say that "refuting these assertions individually is not worth the while." We are confronted here by a really strange fact. Max Dessoir asserts that I say something that, in accordance with my own presuppositions, I would have to label as absurd. It is of course impossible to come to terms with an objection raised by an opponent in this way. One can only recognize and show that a distorted picture was presented as though it were the actual view of the person one is opposing. Now Dessoir might object to this by saying that he could not find in my earlier works any presentation as clear as that in the preceding essay on the conclusions to be drawn from my views on the point at issue here. I admit right away that on many points of anthroposophy my later presentations contain a more exact exposition of what I stated earlier, and that readers of my earlier works can perhaps arrive at an erroneous view here and there of what I myself consider to be the necessary conclusions to be drawn from my views on a certain point. I believe that any insightful person would find this obvious. For, anthroposophy represents a broad field of work, and books can only deal with individual parts of it. But in *this* case can Max Dessoir have recourse to my not having clarified in my earlier books the point at issue here? Dessoir's book was published in 1917. In chapter 6 of the fifth edition of my book *Knowledge of the Higher Worlds and its Attainment*, published in 1914, in the passage dealing with the pictorial manifestation of spiritual experiences in colors, I made the following statement:

> In the descriptions that follow, one must be alert to the fact that "seeing" a color, for example, means a *spiritual seeing* (observing). In clairvoyant knowledge when one says, "I see red," one means, "in the soul-spiritual [realm], I am having an experience that is like the physical experience of the sense impression of the color red." Only because it is completely natural in clairvoyant knowledge in such a case to say "I see red," is this expression used. Someone who is unaware of this fact can easily mistake a color vision for a truly clairvoyant experience.

I added this footnote not because I believed that a reader with true understanding could believe that I assert the possibility of seeing colors without eyes, but because I could imagine that a *superficial* reader here or there, through misunderstanding, could falsely attribute such an assertion to me if I did not expressly state the contrary. Three years later, *after* I had expressly warded off any such imputation, Max Dessoir comes along and declares that I am asserting something that I actually consider to be absurd.

But there is more. In the sixth edition of my book *Theosophy*, also published in 1914, the following statements are made on this subject:

One might picture that what is described here as "color" confronts the soul in the same way a physical color confronts the eye. But any such "soul color" would be nothing but a hallucination. Spiritual science has absolutely nothing to do with "hallucinatory" impressions and they are certainly not what we are referring to in these descriptions. One arrives at a correct picture when one keeps the following in mind. Relative to a *physical color*, the soul *experiences* not only the sense impression, but also has a *soul experience* in connection with it. When the soul perceives a yellow color through the eye, it has a different soul experience than when it perceives a blue color. Let us call this experience "living in yellow" or "living in blue." Now, a soul that has entered the path of knowledge has a similar "experience in yellow" when confronted by the active soul experiences of other entities; and an "experience in blue" when confronted by devotional soul moods. The essential point is not that the "seer," while picturing someone else's soul, sees "blue" the way he sees this "blue" in the physical world, but that he has an experience that justifies him in calling this picture "blue," just as a physical person calls a curtain, for example, "blue." Another *essential* point is that the "seer" is conscious of the fact that, with this experience, he is standing within a body-free experience, and thus is given the possibility of speaking about the value and significance of a soul life in a world whose perception is *not communicated by the human body.*[*]

I will forgo quoting other passages from my books that present my true view on this particular subject. And as to an assessment of Max Dessoir's "version" of my statements, this I leave up to every reader who can still form an objective judgment about the *facts* even when anthroposophy is the topic.

The level of understanding that Dessoir brings to the descriptions I attempted of the consciousness attained through spiritual organs does not bode well for his further presentations on the relation of "Imaginative" pictures to the spiritual reality to which they correspond. He has heard that anthroposophy does not explain the evolution of mankind on earth only by the means employed by anthropology but rather, with its own means, sees this evolution to be dependent upon spiritual powers and beings. In my book *Occult Science, an Outline*, I attempted to make this evolutionary process visible by means of "Imaginative" pictures

---

[*] Please see my book *Theosophy, an Introduction into Knowledge of the Supersensible World and Human Destiny*. In my book *Occult Science, an Outline*, there is a similar presentation about seeing colors. And now we are faced with the unbelievable fact that Max Dessoir cites this book as one of the writings that he supposedly used. *He asserts, therefore, that I say something the exact opposite of which stands in the book he is citing!*

(and through other kinds of knowledge as well that go beyond Imaginative vision, but are not so relevant to our present topic). In that book I indicated how to anthroposophical observation a picture arises of states undergone by mankind in evolutionary forms that are already close to those of the present day; and I also pointed to even earlier evolutionary forms in which the human being appeared that are quite unlike those of today and that are described by me, not in the pictures that anthropology borrows from sense perception, but in Imaginative pictures.

Dessoir then informs his readers in the following way about what I have described as to the evolution of mankind. He says of my depiction of the evolutionary forms that are still close to those of the present-day human being that I designate a specific period of time in the past as the old Indian culture of mankind and then see other cultural periods succeeding it. As Dessoir puts it:

> Old India is not the India we know of today, for, *all* geographic, astronomical, and historical references are to be taken as symbolic. Following the Indian culture, the ancient Persian culture arose, led by Zarathustra who, however, lived much earlier than the historical personality of that name. Other periods followed. We are now in the sixth period.

What I say about a much earlier age of human evolution, in which mankind still appeared in forms quite unlike those of today, is reported by Dessoir like this:

> This human being evolved in a distant past that Steiner calls the Lemurian age of the earth—why in the world?—and in a land that lay then between Australia and India (which, therefore, is an actual place and not a symbol).

31

I want here to totally disregard the fact that I could also see the entire "version" of my description as a mere distortion that could never give the reader a picture of what I mean. I only want to address one point of this "version." Dessoir inspires in his reader the belief that I speak as though what is seen in the spirit is to be taken as symbolic, that old India, therefore, where I locate an ancient culture, is a "symbolic" land. Later, he blames me for locating a much older period of human evolution in Lemuria—between Australia and India—and in doing so contradict myself horribly, since one could notice from my presentation, after all, that I consider Lemuria to be an actual place and not a symbol.

One could only agree fully with the view that a reader of Dessoir's book who has read nothing of my work and only takes up Dessoir's version of it would have to conclude that my presentation is complete rubbish—thoughtless, confused, and self-contradictory.

What *really* stands in my book about the region of the earth I refer to as old India? Read the pertinent passages and you will find that I express with full clarity that old India is not a symbol; it is the region of the earth that basically, if not quite exactly, corresponds with what we all call India. So, Dessoir reports to his reader, as though it were my view, something that it would never even enter my mind to imagine. And because he believes that, in describing old Lemuria, I speak, indeed, in a way that accords with my actual beliefs about old India—but not with the nonsense that *he* ascribes to me—he accuses me of contradiction.

One has to ask oneself how the unbelievable can occur that Dessoir has me assert that old India is to be understood in a *symbolic* way. Out of the whole context of his presentation, I come to the following explanation. Dessoir has read something about the processes in our soul life that I call the path to spiritual vision, whose first level is Imaginative cognition. I describe there how the soul, through calm devotion to certain thoughts, evolves from its own depths the ability to form Imaginative pictures. I say that to this end the soul does best to dwell upon symbolic pictures. No one, through my description, should fall into the error of thinking that these symbolic pictures are anything other than a *means* of arriving at Imaginative cognition. Now, Dessoir believes that, because one arrives at Imaginative picturing by means of symbols, this picturing also consists only in symbolic pictures; indeed, he ascribes to me the view that someone who uses his spiritual organs does not look through the Imaginative pictures at realities, but only at symbols.

With respect to my presentation, Dessoir's assertion that in cases like that of old India I am pointing at symbols, not realities, can only be compared with the following. Someone finds, from the condition of a certain stretch of ground, that in the region where he now is, it must have rained a short while ago. He communicates this to someone else. Naturally, he can only communicate his *mental picture* of the fact that it has rained. Therefore, a third person asserts that the first person is saying that the condition of the ground did not result from real rain, but only from a mental picture of rain. I am asserting neither that Imaginative pictures consist only of mere symbols, nor that they themselves are realities; I am saying that Imaginative pictures relate to a reality the way the mental pictures of ordinary consciousness do. And to impute to me that I am pointing only at symbolic realities is like asserting that the natural scientist does not see the reality to lie within the existence of that to which his mental picture relates, but rather within this picture itself.

When one presents the views one wants to combat the way Dessoir does, the battle is quite easy. And Max Dessoir does make it really easy for himself to sit upon the judge's seat in a lofty manner; but he achieves this only by first perverting my presentations into distorted pictures—often into complete foolishness, in fact—and then scolding his own creation. He states: "It is self-contradictory to say that from 'envisioned' and merely 'symbolic' circumstances, the actual facts of real existence are supposed to have evolved." But you will not find any such self-contradictory way of picturing things in any of my work. Dessoir only imputes such an element to my work. And when he goes so far as to assert: "For the point is not whether one regards the spiritual as brain activity or not, but whether the spiritual is to be regarded in the form of a childish way of picturing things or as a realm with its own lawfulness," then the response must be: I agree with him totally that everything he serves up to his readers as my view bears the mark of a childish way of picturing things; however, what he labels as childish has nothing to do with my real views, but refers totally to his own mental pictures, which he has created by distorting mine.

How is it even possible that a scholar could proceed in this way? In order to contribute toward an answer to this question I must take the reader for a little while into a realm that will perhaps not seem entertaining but that I must enter here in order to show *how Max Dessoir reads the books* that he appoints himself to judge. I must bring a little philology to bear upon Max Dessoir's presentations.

As already mentioned, Dessoir describes my picture of the evolution of human cultural periods within certain time frames as follows: "The Old Persian culture followed the Old Indian. Other periods of time succeeded them. We are now in the sixth period." Now it might seem quite petty to criticize someone for having me say that we are now in the *sixth* period whereas I actually show, with all possible clarity, that we are in the *fifth* period. But in this case the matter is not such an insignificant one. For, anyone who has penetrated into the whole spirit of my presentation of this subject would have to admit that someone to whom it would even occur to believe I was speaking of the sixth period as our present one must have misunderstood my whole presentation in the grossest manner. My designation of the present period as the *fifth* is intimately connected with my whole discussion of this topic.

How did Dessoir arrive at his gross misunderstanding? One can form a picture of this if one compares my presentation of the matter with his "version" of it and, in doing so, tests it by the philological method.

When, in my description of the cultural epoch, I arrive at the *fourth* period—which I see to begin in the eighth century BC and end in about the fourteenth or fifteenth century—I say the following:

In the fourth, fifth, and sixth centuries AD, a cultural era spread over Europe in which we are still living today. It was meant to gradually replace the fourth epoch, the Greco-Roman. It is the fifth Post-Atlantean cultural epoch.

Accordingly, my view is that, through processes occurring in the fourth, fifth, and *sixth* centuries, effects were prepared that needed several centuries more to ripen, in order then, in the fourteenth century, to make the transition into the *fifth* cultural epoch in which we are still living now. In his reading of the above passage, Max Dessoir seems to have brought it into the domain of his attention in such a way that he *confused* the sequence of the fourth, *fifth*, and *sixth* centuries with the sequence of the cultural epochs. When someone reads superficially and in addition has no understanding of what he is reading, such things can occur.

I would not advance this hypothesis about Max Dessoir's superficiality by itself if it were not supported by the following discoveries that one can make in his "version" of my presentations. In order to discuss the pertinent factors here, I must introduce mental pictures relative to anthroposophical knowledge that are hardly comprehensible if not viewed in connection with the presentations in my book *Occult Science, an Outline* that refer to them. I myself would never tear them out of all context and introduce them to a reader or listener the way Dessoir does. But since he bases his criticism on his "version" of views that in my presentations are in a broad context, I must address this "version" here. I must show what kind of "version" this is. To begin with I must note that the depiction of such matters presents such difficulties because the content of spiritual observation can only be elucidated to some extent when one strives for the most exact possible forms of expression. Therefore, when presenting such matters, I always try to spare myself no pains or time in struggling to attain the greatest possible exactitude in my form of verbal expression. Anyone who penetrates even a little way into the spirit of anthroposophy will understand what I have just said.

In the light of this, let me now show how Max Dessoir proceeds in giving his "version" of my presentations.*

With respect to the path that the soul takes in order to acquire the use of its soul organs, he presents my views in the following way:

The schooling toward a higher state of consciousness begins—at least for a human being of today—
with his immersing himself with all his strength into a
mental picture as though into a purely soul state of
affairs. A symbolic mental picture works best, such as
the visualization of a black cross (symbol of annihilated lower drives and passions), whose crossing
point is circumscribed by seven red roses (symbol of
purified drives and passions).

Leaving aside the fact that this statement, torn out of context, must make a strange impression upon a reader,

---

* One could perhaps point to something here that is not taken into consideration in those circles that often want to judge anthroposophical endeavors in terms of their philosophical and scientific validity. I do not want to leave out this point, because the opinion could easily arise in some people that what I am bringing against Dessoir is a much too pedantic insistence upon my actual words. In anthroposophy we are dealing with descriptions of the spiritual. In doing so, one must use the words and even the word combinations of ordinary language. But it is absolutely the case that one cannot always find adequate terminology for that toward which the soul directs its attention when it observes something spiritual. The relationships that hold sway in the spiritual realm and the particular nature of what one can call the beings and occurrences there are much more complicated, subtle, and manifold than what comes to expression in our ordinary use of language. One attains the goal only if one avails oneself of the linguistic potential of sentence structure and word transformation, and if one strives to bring to expression through a second sentence—*in connection with* the first—something that one cannot adequately express in one sentence. To understand anthroposophy it is absolutely necessary to enter into such matters. The case can arise, for example, that a spiritual state of affairs is seen in a completely skewed way if the *form of expression* is not regarded as essential to it. Dessoir has not even come close to recognizing the need to take such things into consideration. He seems to assume everywhere that what is incomprehensible to him is based upon childish thinking and the primitive method of the other person.

whereas this would hardly be the case if read at its proper place in my book, I must say that, if I read what Max Dessoir states in the above sentence as the opinion of some person, I would consider the whole matter as nonsense, or at least as nonsensically expressed. For, I could find no connection between the meanings of the two symbols, between "annihilated lower drives and passions" and "purified drives and passions." I would, in fact, have to picture that a person is supposed to annihilate his lower drives and passions, and then, at the place where the annihilation occurred, purified drives and passions arise as though shooting forth out of nothingness. But why "purified," since there is nothing there to "purify"; something new has arisen at the place of the annihilation? In no way could my thinking deal with such a statement. But read what I wrote in my book. I say:

Picture a black cross to yourself. Let this be a *symbol* for the annihilated lower element of our drives and passions; and there, where the two arms cross, picture to yourself seven red, radiant roses in a circle.

You can see that I do *not* say that the cross is a symbol for "annihilated lower drives," but for the "annihilated lower elements of our drives and passions." So, the lower drives and passions are not "annihilated," but rather "transformed," in such a way that their lower element is cast off and they themselves manifest as purified. This is how Max Dessoir deals with something that he wants to critique. Then he can portray it as a childish way of picturing things. It is definitely pedantic to correct someone's formulations in this pedagogical manner. But I am not the instigator of this pedagogical act. It is Dessoir's distortions, which can only be caught by the pedagogical approach, that make it neces-

sary. For these distortions amount to misrepresentations—
which, as far as I am concerned, arose unconsciously or
through superficiality—of my own actual formulations.
And *only* with respect to these misrepresentations is Dessoir's critique possible.

Here is another example of Dessoir's "version" of what
he reads. I speak—again, in a context that makes the matter
appear completely different than when torn out of context
in the Dessoirian manner—of certain earlier stages of the
earth's evolution before it became a planet inhabitable by
man in his present form of development. In Imaginative
mental pictures I describe the first stage of this evolution. In
order to elucidate these periods I have to speak of beings of
a spiritual nature who were connected with the primal
planetary form of the earth at that time. After Dessoir has
me assert that through these spiritual beings "processes of
nutrition and excretion develop" upon the planetary primal
form of the earth, he continues: "A clairvoyant person still
experiences these states today through a supersensible perception that is like smell, for these states are actually still
present today." What you will read in my book is that the
relevant spiritual beings enter into interaction with "forces
of taste that billow up and down" within the inner being of
the primal planetary form. "As a result, its etheric or life
body unfolds an activity of such a sort that one could call it
a kind of metabolism." Then I say that these beings bring
life into the inner entity of this primal planetary form.
"Processes of nutrition and excretion occur as a result." It is
obvious that sharpest rejection of such a description by
present-day science is possible. But it should be just as
obvious that a critic cannot go about his work the way Max
Dessoir does. While awakening the belief that he is repro-

ducing my description, he says that processes of nutrition and excretion develop through the beings referred to. The way I describe the matter, between my indication that beings arise and the indication that nutritional and excretory processes arise, there is an intermediary statement to the effect that an interaction develops and that through *it* an activity arises in the etheric or life body of these beings that now in its turn leads to the nutritional and excretory processes of the primal planetary form. What Dessoir accomplishes with my description can be compared with the following. Someone says: "A man enters a room in which a child and its father are present. The child treats the visitor in such a way that the father must punish him." Another person now misrepresents this statement by asserting: "The punishment of the child arises from the visit of the stranger." Now, from this assertion, could anyone know what the first person actually wanted to say? Nevertheless, Dessoir has me say in addition that the clairvoyant learns about certain conditions, arising in the primal planetary form, "through a perception that is like smelling." But my formulation is that, in the relevant states, will forces manifest that communicate themselves "to clairvoyant perception through effects that can be compared with 'odor.'" So, in my work, there is no trace of an assertion that the spiritual perception under discussion is "like smelling"; rather, the fact emerges quite clearly that this perception is *not* like smelling, but that what is perceived *can be compared* to odors. How such a comparison is to be understood in an anthroposophical sense is amply demonstrated at another place in this book. Nevertheless, through this misrepresentation of my formulation, Dessoir gives himself an opening for the following remark, which he probably considers clever: "I am surprised that the 'odor of sanctity' is not connected here with the 'stench of the devil.' "

I could now present (and rectify) more examples like these of Dessoir's "versions" of my presentations, such as the way he has me explain the "going to sleep" of a leg "through separation of the etheric body from the physical body," whereas I do *not* explain in that way the *objective* fact of a "leg going to sleep," but rather state that the subjective "strange sensation that one feels" results "from the separation of the etheric body." Only if one takes my *formulations the way they are given, can one form an opinion as to the significance of my statements* and recognize how they absolutely do not exclude the objective facts discovered by natural science, anymore than they need to be excluded by the adherent of anthropological views. Dessoir, however, wants to make his readers believe that my views should be excluded from scientific consideration. But I need not tire the reader any longer with such corrections. I only wanted to show the degree of superficiality with which Max Dessoir reads what he sets himself up to judge.

But I still want to show where that soul attitude can lead that sits in judgment with such superficiality. In my book *The Spiritual Guidance of Man and Mankind*, I try to show how the power to make mental pictures—which does not enter the *consciousness* of the child right away at birth but only at an older age—is already active before it emerges consciously, and how in its unconscious activity (in the upbuilding of the nervous system, for example, and in other ways), this power works in such a wisdom-filled way, that its later conscious working seems much less wise by comparison. For reasons too extensive to present here, I arrive at the view that our conscious life of mental picturing does indeed develop further the wisdom active in early child-hood in certain formations of the human organism, but that this conscious life of mental pictures relates to that uncon-scious working of wisdom the way, for example, the struc-ture of a tool stemming from conscious human wisdom relates to the marvelous structure of the human brain. The reader of the above-mentioned book can easily see from it that I do not express any such statement as the result of a sudden "inspiration," in an anthroposophical sense, even though I of course cannot present in *every* book the details of this path. In this respect I must ask that my books be consid-ered as parts of one whole that mutually support and carry one another. But my concern now is not with presenting the validity of my statement about unconscious or conscious wisdom, but with something else that Dessoir does by re-tailoring the relevant passage of my book for his readers in the following way: "Our connection with the higher worlds—we read—is closest in our first three years of life, to which no memory extends. Especially a person who himself teaches wisdom—as *Mr. Rudolf Steiner* confesses—will say to himself: 'As a child I worked upon myself through powers that worked in from the spiritual worlds, and what I can now give as my best must also work in from higher worlds; I must not regard it as belonging to my ordinary consciousness.' "

One might well ask: what picture imprints itself in a reader of Dessoir's book whose eye falls upon these sen-tences? Hardly anything other than that, in this book, I gave myself occasion to speak of the connection of the spiritual world to the knowing human being, and present myself as an example. It is obviously not difficult to expose someone to ridicule whom one can reproach with such bad taste. But what is the actual state of affairs? My book states:

42

Imagine that a person has found adherents, a few people who acknowledge him. Such a person, through genuine self-knowledge, can easily become aware that precisely the fact that he has found adherents gives him the feeling that what he has to say does not originate from him. It is much more the case that spiritual powers from higher worlds wish to communicate with his adherents and find in the teacher the suitable instrument through which to reveal themselves.

The thought will occur to such a person: As a child, I worked upon myself through powers that worked in from the spiritual world, and what I can now give as my best must also work in from higher worlds; I must not regard it as belonging to my ordinary consciousness. Yes, such a person may say that something "demonic," something like a "daimon"—but a "daimon" in the sense of a good spiritual power—is working from a spiritual world through me upon my adherents.

Socrates experienced something like this.... Many efforts have been made to explain this "daimon" of Socrates. But one can explain it only if one wishes to give oneself over to the thought that Socrates was able to feel something like what is described in the above discussion.

You can see that the issue for me is to grasp the Socratic "daimon" from the anthroposophical point of view. There are many views about this Socratic "daimon." One can find grounds for opposing my view just as well as these other views. But what does Max Dessoir do? Where I speak of Socrates, he twists the matter to seem that I am speaking about myself by stating, "as Mr. Rudolf Steiner confesses" and even putting my name in italics. What are we dealing with here? With nothing less, in fact, than an *objective untruth*. I leave it up to any fair thinker to form a judgment about a critic who employs such means.

But the matter does not end there. For, after using my view of the Socratic "daimon" in the way just described, Dessoir writes further:

> The fact, therefore, that the individual person is the bearer of supra-individual truths coarsens here to the picture that a spirit world, conceived as thing-like, is connected with the individual person by pipes or wires, so to speak: Hegel's objective spirit transforms itself into a group of demons and all the shadow shapes of an impure religious thinking arise again. The whole direction characterizes itself as a materialistic coarsening of soul processes and as a personifying leveling of spiritual values.

In the face of such "critique," all possibility of serious discussion with the critic really ends. Just reflect what we have before us here. I speak of the "daimon" of Socrates, about which Socrates himself has spoken, according to historical references. Max Dessoir imputes to me the view that when one speaks of the demonic in this way, then "Hegel's objective spirit transforms itself into a group of demons ...." So Dessoir uses his strange deviation from the thoughts as they were truly meant, to instill in his reader the view that someone is justified in assuming about me that I see in Hegel's objective spirit "a group of demons."

Just place beside this Dessoirian assertion all that I present in my book *The Riddles of Philosophy* to keep at a distance from Hegel's view of the "objective spirit" everything that could possibly stamp this spirit with the character of

44

the demonic. Anyone who, with respect to what I have presented about Hegel, would say that the proponent of anthroposophy has mental pictures by which Hegel's "objective spirit" transforms itself into a group of demons, any such person would be asserting an objective untruth. For, he cannot even hide behind the excuse that: Yes, Steiner does in fact present it differently, but I can only imagine that the Steinerian anthroposophical presuppositions lead to the conclusions I have just drawn. To say this, in fact, would only show that he is not in a position to understand my presentations on Hegel's "objective spirit." After making his jump from Socrates to Hegel, Max Dessoir judges on: "Out of an inability to understand in accordance with the facts there spring forth these fantasies that are not inhibited by any scientific scruples...."

Whoever reads my books and then looks at Dessoir's representation of my views might perhaps feel, when confronted by such a statement, that I have some right to give it the following turn: From Max Dessoir, out of his inability to understand, in accordance with the facts, what I say in my books, there spring forth the most superficial, objectively untrue fantasies about the mental pictures of anthroposophy.

Max Dessoir shares with his readers the fact that besides my *Occult Science, an Outline,* he has also "used a long series of other writings." From the way his manner of "expressing" himself has been characterized here, one can hardly ascertain what he means by "using a long series" of my writings. I looked into the chapter on anthroposophy in his book to see which of my books—besides *Occult Science, an Outline*—show traces of "use." I can only discover that this "long series" consists of three small books: *The Spiritual*

Guidance of Man and Mankind, consisting of 64 pages; *Blood Is a Very Special Fluid,* a reprint of a lecture that takes up all of 48 small pages; and the 46-page booklet *Reincarnation and Karma.* In addition he mentions *The Philosophy of Spiritual Activity* (1894) in a footnote. However much it might go against my grain to respond to this footnote with a few purely personal remarks, I must still do so, because even such incidental matters display Max Dessoir's own particular level of scientific exactitude. He states: "In Steiner's first work *The Philosophy of Spiritual Activity* (Berlin 1894), only germs of his actual teachings are to be found..." Max Dessoir calls *The Philosophy of Spiritual Activity* my "first" work (*Erstling*). The truth is that my literary activity began with my introductions to Goethe's natural-scientific writings, the first volume of which appeared in 1883, i.e., eleven years before the date set by Dessoir for my "first" work. Preceding this "first" work are the extensive introductions to three volumes of Goethe's natural-scientific works, my *Science of Knowing* (1886), my book *Goethe As Father of a New Aesthetics* (1889), and *Truth and Science* (1892), which lays the foundation for my whole world view. I would not have mentioned this further case of Dessoir's strange apprehension of what he writes about if the fact were not that all the basic views contained in *The Philosophy of Spiritual Activity* were already expressed in my earlier books and only *re*presented them in a way that synthesized them and came to terms with the philosophical-epistemological views of the end of the nineteenth century. In *The Philosophy of Spiritual Activity* I wished to express, in a systematic, organic form, what I had written in the previous (almost entire) decade of extensive publications of epistemological groundwork and its ethical-philo-

46

sophical implications for a view aiming at a grasp of the spiritual world.

After writing in this way about my "first" work, Max Dessoir continues to speak about it:

> It is stated there that man has taken over into himself something from nature, and therefore through knowledge of his own being, can solve the riddle of nature; that, in thinking, a creative activity precedes knowing, whereas we are not involved in the coming about of nature and so are dependent on knowing it subsequently. Intuition counts here merely as the form in which a thought content at first appears.

Look and see whether there is anything in *The Philosophy of Spiritual Activity* that could be synthesized into such monstrously trivial statements. In my book, after an extensive discussion of other philosophical directions, I tried to show that, for man, full reality is not present to sense observation, that the world picture given by the senses, therefore, is an incomplete reality. I made every effort to demonstrate that the human organization causes this incompletenes. Nature does not hide from man what is missing from the sense-perceptible picture as its essential being; rather *man* is so constituted that through this constitution, at the level merely observational knowing, he hides from himself the spiritual side of his world picture. In active thinking then, the opening up of this spiritual side begins. In active thinking, according to my world view, something real (spiritual) is *directly present* that cannot yet be given to mere observation. That is precisely what characterizes my epistemological foundation for a spiritual science: that in intuition—insofar as it comes to expression in thinking—I do *not* see "merely the forms in which a thought content at first appears." So Max Dessoir wishes to present his readers with *the opposite* of what is actually expressed in *The Philosophy of Spiritual Activity.*

In order to see this, you need only look at the following thoughts from that book:

> In thinking we are given the element that joins our particular individuality into one whole with the cosmos. Insofar as we sense and feel (and also perceive) we are separate entities; insofar as we think, we are the all-one-being that permeates everything .... The perception, therefore, is nothing finished, closed off; it is one side of total reality. The other side is the concept. The act of knowledge is the synthesis of perception and concept .... In contrast to the content of perception, which is given to us from outside, thought content appears in our inner being. Let us call the form in which thought content at first arises "intuition." It is for thinking what *observation is* for perceptions. Intuition and observation are the sources of our knowledge.

So, I say here: I wish to use "intuition" as an *expression* for the form in which the spiritual reality anchored in the thought content *at first* appears in the human soul, before the soul has recognized that in this conceptual inner experience there is contained the side of reality that is not yet given in the perception. Therefore, I say that intuition "is for thinking what *observation* is for perceptions." So even when Max Dessoir *seemingly* presents someone's thoughts verbatim, he is able to twist what the other person means into its opposite. Dessoir has me say "Intuition counts here *merely* as the form in which a thought content at first appears." He leaves out the following sentence, which makes nonsense of his use of the word "merely." For me, intuition counts not "*merely*" as the "form in which a thought content at first appears," but as the revelation of a spiritual-real element, just as the perception is a revelation of a material-real element. If I say "My watch appears at first as the content of my vest pocket; it measures time for me," someone else cannot assert that I said: "The watch is '*merely*' the content of my vest pocket."

In the context of what I have published, *The Philosophy of Spiritual Activity* lays the epistemological foundation for the anthroposophically oriented spiritual science advocated by me. I explained this in the last chapter of my book *The Riddles of Philosophy*. I showed there how, in my view, a path leads straight from *Truth and Science* and *The Philosophy of Spiritual Activity* to anthroposophy. But Max Dessoir, through his non-use of my two-volume book, *The Riddles of Philosophy*, creates for himself the possibility of telling his readers all kinds of easily misunderstood stories about the "long series" of my three small books *The Spiritual Guidance of Man and Mankind*, *Blood Is a Very Special Fluid*, and *Reincarnation and Karma*. In the first little book, I try to recognize how the powers of concrete spiritual beings are at work in the course of the spiritual development of mankind. I made it clear to my readers (at least I thought I did) that I am very conscious of how easily the content of precisely this book could be misunderstood. In the preface I state expressly that someone who picks up this book without having the prerequisite background would have to "regard it as the curious product of pure fantasy." To be sure, in this preface I name only the content of *Theosophy* and *Occult Science, An Outline* as prerequisites. That was in 1911. In 1914 my book *The Riddles of Philosophy* was published as the second edition of my two-volume book *Nineteenth-Century Views of Life and the World* (1900 and 1901). In *The Riddles of Philosophy* I also described how the atomic theory arose and how researchers like Galileo (in my view) fit into the course of mankind's development; in this description, I did not refer to anything other than what is "clearly evident to everyone" relative to the origins of the atomic theory or Galileo's place in the history of science.[*]

My presentation, to be sure, is made in my own way; but in *this* presentation I refer to nothing other than is usual in any presentation of an outline of the history of philosophy. In my book *The Spiritual Guidance of Man and Mankind* the attempt I made was to show how that which I myself strove in another book to show as "evident to everyone" is the result of the powers of concrete spiritual beings at work in the course of human development. Taken out of its context in *The Spiritual Guidance of Man and Mankind*, the relevant thought (in my opinion) can only be rendered in the following way: In the spiritual history of mankind, besides the forces that ordinary historical methods have found to be "clearly evident to everyone," there are other powers (supersensible beings) working as well that are accessible only to spiritual-scientific research. And the powers of these beings work in accordance with specific, knowable laws. In the way in which man's cognitive powers work in that developmental period of mankind which I call the Egypto-Chaldean (from the fourth to the first pre-Christian millennium), one can recognize the powers of those beings who arise

---

[*] I also spoke of Galileo in the introductions and annotations to Goethe's natural-scientific works (*Goethean Science*).

again in the age in which the atomic theory originates, but in a different form of activity. In the arising and further development of atomism I see those powers of spiritual beings at work that were already at work in a different way in the mode of thinking during the Egypto-Chaldean age.

Even someone who only goes into my books in a quite cursory way can find that through my anthroposophic viewpoint I do not assert the existence of spiritual powers at work in the course of man's development in order to obscure purely historical observations with all kinds of anthropomorphisms or analogies or in order to shift them into the twilight dimness of some false mysticism. Max Dessoir finds it possible, with respect to our topic here, to present his readers with these words:

> No! Here even the most patient reporter can no longer hold his peace. It is evident to everyone how the atomic theory arose and developed consequentially since antiquity, and now someone comes along and calls for help from the mysterious great unknown!

Whoever reads *The Riddles of Philosophy* can see that what is evident to everyone is also presented by me in the way it is evident to everyone: and that—for those who are able to understand that what is evident to everyone contains something that is not evident to everyone—I am pointing to this something, which is accessible to spiritual vision. And I am not pointing to a "mysterious unknown," but to something in fact that is *known* through the anthroposophical viewpoint." [*]

---

[*] Please forgive me for borrowing from mathematics an analogy for the Dessoirian kind of critique. Suppose that, in the context of logarithms someone says: two numbers are multiplied when you add their logarithms and seek the antilogarithm of their sum as their product. Then someone

I have shown that it is inadmissible for Max Dessoir to twist my reference to Socrates to mean that I was speaking of myself. But it is clear from the context that Max Dessoir is referring to none other than himself in his comment on page 34 of his book. In order to understand this comment, one must note that Dessoir distinguishes between two regions in the moment of consciousness: between a central field and a peripheral zone. He expounds on how the contents of consciousness move continuously from one of these regions to the other. It is only that these contents take on a particular appearance when they enter the peripheral zone. They lose sharpness, show fewer characteristics than usual, and become indistinct. The peripheral zone leads a marginal existence. But there are two ways that they attain independent activity. The first way does not pertain here. Dessoir expresses himself as follows about the second way:

> The other kind of independence occurs in such a way that the peripheral zone does indeed remain as a *co-consciousness beside the main consciousness*, but lifts itself to a greater distinctness and coherency of its content and enters thereby into a completely new relation to the simultaneous fully conscious soul activity. To use another easily grasped picture: a complex glides from the center of a circle to the periphery, but does not sink into obscurity there but rather partly preserves its distinctness and coherency.

In connection with this, Dessoir then states:

> An example: When I am lecturing on very familiar trains of thoughts, it sometimes happens to me

comes along and says: "No! Everyone knows how numbers are multiplied and here is a person talking about addition!" Max Dessoir's critique is of this sort in the above case.

that my concepts and words end up in that region and my attention occupies itself with other things. In spite of that, I speak on, without the participation of my consciousness, as it were. When this happens the following sometimes occurs: I am surprised by a sudden silence in the room and have to be reminded that it is due to the fact that I myself have stopped talking! Habitual mental connections and judgments, therefore, can also be made subconsciously, sometimes even those that move along invisibly; the movements of the organs of speech connected with them also run their course without difficulty in their usual groove.

To be sure, if I draw the full implications of this passage, I would rather believe that they do not refer to Dessoir's own experience but rather to something that he noticed in other absent-minded lecturers, and that he is only using the words "me" and "I" stylistically as though he were putting himself in someone else's place. The context in which these sentences occur makes this explanation difficult, to be sure, and possible only if one assumes that a stylistic device got in under Dessoir's guard, which does happen to many writers in our hurried times.

But however the case may be, the essential point is that a state of soul in which the "subconscious" plays a role like that just described in Dessoir's lecturer is the very first thing that must be overcome in the soul if a person wants to penetrate to an understanding of anthroposophical knowledge. The exact opposite—the thorough permeating of concepts with consciousness—is necessary if these concepts are to have a relation to the genuine spiritual world. In the sphere of anthroposophy a speaker who continues to speak when his "attention" is occupied "with other things" is an impossibility. For, someone who wants to grasp anthroposophy must have accustomed himself to not separating the direction of his attention from the direction of a train of thought that he is evoking. He will not go on speaking of things from which he has withdrawn his attention because he will no longer be thinking about these things.

But if I only look at the way Max Dessoir reports to his readers on my little book *Blood is a Very Special Fluid*, the thought does occur to me that he not only *speaks on* when his attention turns to "other things," but in such a state actually *writes on*. In his report you will find the following. My statement is quoted that our "blood takes up the pictures of the outer world that our brain has inwardized," and then Dessoir adds the comment:

> This kind of monstrous ignoring of all facts combines with the assertion—just as unprovable as it is incomprehensible—that prehistoric man, in the "pictures that his blood received," also remembered the experiences of his ancestors.

But if one reads in context the sentences that Dessoir quotes and put beside them the comment on the same page—"I must speak in analogies if I want to present the complicated processes that pertain here"—then one will perhaps understand in fact what it means when someone reports the way Dessoir does.

Picture what it would be like if I were writing about Max Dessoir's *Beyond the Soul* and told my readers: And now someone comes along and asserts that the blood "running in our veins" is "the blood of many millennia." This is just as unprovable as it is incomprehensible and has the same value as another assertion: "But beyond any doubt, behind the surface of our consciousness there is a dark, richly-filled space, whose changes also change the curvature of the surface." These two sentences are in Dessoir's book, the second on page 1 and the first, about the "blood of millennia," on page 12. Both sentences, of course, are fully justified because Max Dessoir is expressing himself "in analogies." When I *have to* do the same and expressly state so, Dessoir forges for himself a critical weapon out of wooden iron to refute me.

Dessoir states that my reference to spiritual being, "on the whole, characterizes itself as a materialistic coarsening of soul processes and as an anthropomorphic leveling of spiritual values." With respect to the contents of my books, this assertion makes about as much sense as the following would make: "A thinker who is capable of saying that 'to use an admittedly very imperfect analogy, one can call the present moment of consciousness a circle, whose circumference is black, whose center is white, and whose intermediary areas are gradations of gray,' such a thinker's view characterizes itself 'on the whole … as a materialistic coarsening of soul processes.' And the thinker who is doing this grotesque thing—comparing the present moment of consciousness with a circle and speaking of white, gray, and black—is Max Dessoir." Now it would of course never occur to me to say such things, because I know that Max Dessoir in this case is not coarsening soul processes in a materialistic manner. But what *he* does to me *is like what I have just hypothetically characterized.*

You can see the total impossibility of discussing the meaning of the law of destiny from an anthroposophical viewpoint with a critic who bases himself on presuppositions like those of a Dessoir; I would have to cite whole chapters from my books here to show Dessoir's hair-raising distortions of my descriptions of human destiny when he says:

> Here, supposedly, a connection between cause and effect in the spiritual world is revealed (so causality does not pertain only to the phenomenal world as grasped by the intellect). A person who perfects himself through a series of lifetimes is subject to the law of karma, according to which every deed brings its inevitable effects along with it; thus, for example, one's present poverty is one's own fault from an earlier life.

In 1887, in my introduction to the second volume of Goethe's natural-scientific work, I wrote:

> The explaining of a process in nature is a going back to its determining factors: a seeking out of the producer in addition to the product that is given. When I perceive an effect and then seek its cause, these two perceptions do not by any means satisfy my need for explanation. I must go back to the laws by which *this* cause brings forth *this* effect. It is different with human action. Here the lawfulness that determines a phenomenon itself enters into action; that which makes a product itself appears upon the scene of activity. We have to do with a manifesting existence at which we can remain, for which we do not need to ask about deeper-lying determining factors.*

It is perfectly clear what I mean: One cannot ask about the determining factors of a human action in the same way as with a process of nature. So there must be a difference.

---

* Please see page 151 of *Goethean Science*. Ed.

Therefore, my views about destiny connections, which are closely related to those about the sources of human will, cannot refer to the relation between cause and effect spoken of in natural science. For this reason, in my book *Theosophy*, I took every pain to make clear that I am far from thinking that the experiences of one life work over into subsequent ones the way cause and effect work in nature. Max Dessoir distorts my picture of destiny in the crudest way by weaving into his report of it the statement: "So causality does not pertain only to the phenomenal world as grasped by the intellect."

He creates for himself the possibility of adding this comment only by lifting out of my little book *Reincarnation and Karma* a statement that sums up a lengthier discussion. But only this discussion gives this statement its rightful meaning. The isolated form in which Dessoir presents this statement opens it to cheap criticism. The statement reads:

Everything that I have the ability for and actually do in my present life does not stand there isolated and alone as some kind of miracle, but it is connected with my soul's earlier forms of existence as effect, and with its later forms as cause.

Anyone who goes so far as to read this statement in the context of the discussion that it sums up will find that I understand the working over of *one* form of life into the *other* in such a way that one cannot put it in the category of causality in the usual, purely natural-scientific sense. One can only use the abbreviated term "causality" in a broader sense if one explains exactly what one means by it or if one can safely assume that the reader already knows how the word is being used. What precedes my summing-up sentence, however, will not allow this sentence to be understood in any other way than:

Everything that I have the ability for and actually do in my present life is connected, as effect, with my soul's earlier forms of existence to the extent that the causes (lying *in my present life*) of my abilities and actions relate to the other forms of my life in a kind of connection that is not causality in the ordinary sense; and everything that I have the ability for and actually do is connected with my soul's later forms of existence to the extent that these abilities and deeds are the cause of effects in my present life that now in their turn relate to the content of later forms of my life in a kind of connection that again is not causality in the ordinary sense.

Anyone who investigates my writings will see that I have never advocated a concept of karma that is incompatible with the picture of man's free being. Dessoir could have noticed this fact even if he had not "used" more of my writings than what stands in my *Occult Science, An Outline*:

Anyone who believes that human freedom is not compatible with predetermination of the future configuration of things should reflect that man's free action in the future depends just as little upon how the predetermined things will be, as freedom depends upon the fact that he plans in one year to live in the house whose blueprints he is drawing up now.

For even if these statements do not relate directly to the circumstances of human earthly lives, still, someone could not write them who believes that the destinies of our earthly lives relate to each other in a way that corresponds to the law of causality in the natural-scientific sense.

58

Nowhere in Dessoir's book can one see that he made any effort to investigate the way I build the epistemological and general philosophical foundation—in accordance also with natural-scientific views—of the anthroposophy advocated by me. Instead, he makes assertions that do not have even *distant* reference points in my writings. For example, on page 296f. of his book, he writes:

> We hear that medieval medicine—still totally under this spell—divided up man according to the zodiac and saw in the hand with its fingers subdivisions of the heaven's proportions. Or we read in Rudolf Steiner that before fertilization the plant is in the same situation that the whole earth was before its separation from the sun. These are examples of the basic principle of seeing in small things a copy of great cosmic processes.*

But even if Max Dessoir's statements were just as correct as they are actually false they would still serve the purpose of lumping my anthroposophical viewpoint together with all kinds of dilettantish goings-on that manifest today as mysticism, theosophy, and the like. In reality, this assertion of Dessoir's—all by itself—proves fully that this

---

* Max Dessoir writes this in reference to statements at the end of *Occult Science, An Outline*. He has not even come close to understanding what I said there. Otherwise the thought could never have occurred to him that the matter could have anything at all to do with his dilettantish method of seeking "correspondences" between widely separated facts. Any unprejudiced person must see that what I say about the separation of the sun and earth on the one hand and fertilization of the plant on the other can be discovered in a completely independent way, *without* setting out to discover "correspondences." One could just as well say that the physicist is seeking "correspondences" when he investigates the polar-opposite facts of the anode and cathode. But Max Dessoir is far from understanding that the method employed by me has nothing to do with what he is attacking, but rather is totally in the *mode of a natural-scientific thinking applied to the realm of spirit*.

critic approaches my anthroposophy without any understanding either for its philosophical foundation or its methods—or even, in fact, for the *form of expression* of its results. Basically, Dessoir's critique is no different than many other "responses" to which the anthroposophy advocated by me is prey. Coming to terms with them is unfruitful because they do not critique what they claim to be judging, but rather a caricature arbitrarily drawn by them that is then quite easy to attack. It seems quite impossible to me that anyone who sees what I value in anthroposophy could put it, as Dessoir does, together with a literary, unintended burlesque like the *Faust* books of J. A. Louvier, with the repulsive racial mysticism of Guido List, with Christian Science, or even with everything that Dessoir calls "Neo-Buddhism."

I leave it up to those who really want to learn to know my books to judge whether Max Dessoir is justified in saying of them:

> It betrays an undemanding thinking when someone requires merely that the reader acknowledge what he is reading, as not contrary to reason (for, in a broader sense, much is possible that remains improbable and fruitless); or when things are nowhere investigated, questioned, doubted, or weighed but only dictated from on high in the form, "occult science says such and such."

Or what about a statement like: "Unsuspecting readers might be taken in by the examples sprinkled about or by the purported explanations of certain experiences ...." It can at best make me think that "unsuspecting readers" of Dessoir's book might be taken in by the quotations from my books that Dessoir sprinkles about and interprets nonsensically or by the nice trivializing of my thoughts.

If, in spite of the fruitlessness to which a discussion with this critic is doomed *from the beginning*, I nevertheless undertake one here, it is because I *had* to show once again, with an example, the kind of judgment encountered by what I call anthroposophy; and because there are altogether too many "unsuspecting readers" who form judgments about such a spiritual striving from books like Dessoir's without acquainting themselves with what is being judged, and without even an inkling of the true nature of what is being caricatured for them.

I will also not judge, but leave it up to the readers of my books to judge, what significance it has when someone like Dessoir, who is far from understanding my goals and who reads the books he is judging the way he does, asserts "from on high" that I "care about certain connections with science," but possess "no inner relation to the spirit of science."

It would almost have been a miracle for Max Dessoir's whole approach for him not to have added to everything else the statement: "Indeed the bulk of his disciples renounce fully any work of their own in thinking." How often do those people have to hear this (whom one likes to call my "disciples")! Certainly there are "disciples" of dubious character in every spiritual endeavor. But the point is whether *they* and not others perhaps are characteristic of the endeavor. What does Max Dessoir know about my "disciples"? What does he know about the number of them who are not only far from renouncing any work of their own in thinking but who—after recognizing through their work in thinking the scientific inadequacy of world views of the stripe of Dessoir's—do not disdain to draw impulses from

61

endeavors by which, as well as I can, I am seeking a methodical path by which to penetrate a little way into the spiritual world. Perhaps a time is also coming when one will judge more correctly those present-day people who can accomplish *enough* work in thinking not to belong to Max Dessoir's "unsuspecting readers."*,**

---

* Only the fact that Dessoir is in no position to really form an adequate picture of anthroposophical striving can explain why he cannot enter with understanding for these strivings, even into areas very close to where his own train of thought lands him. A case in point is the area he points to in two sentences from his book: "There is nothing beyond the soul in the sense of an invisible reality, because the spiritual state of affairs is raised above the existence of things as well as of persons. What is objectively beyond the soul may be regarded as a supra-consciousness, but never as something existing spatially outside the soul." Dessoir does not see that with such statements he does not provide a refutation, but rather a precise proof of the necessity for anthroposophy. He does not see that everywhere in my books the attempt is made to treat the relevant questions as *questions of consciousness*. Please take note of how *this attempt* is carried through precisely in my *Occult Science, an Outline*, for example. But Dessoir just cannot see that through this the whole cognitive process, with respect to the spiritual world, is made into an inner function of consciousness and that, *within* consciousness itself, other forms of consciousness must be sought in an experiential way that are not concerned in fact with "something existing spatially outside the soul," but are concerned with the soul's presence within an existent something that is nonspatial in exactly the same sense as the experiences of ordinary consciousness themselves are already nonspatial. To be sure, someone who wants to understand this must be able to do justice in an anthroposophical sense to a statement like that of Friedrich Theodor Vischer in the first part of his book *Old and New* (*Altes und Neues*): "The soul, to be sure, as the uppermost unity of all processes, cannot be localized in the body, even though it is nowhere else than in the body..." This statement belongs to those that lead to the borderland of our ordinary knowing, in the sense of chapter 1 of this book and in the sense of Addendum 1 of "Sketches of Some of the Ramifications of the Content of this Book" on page 107: "The Philosophical Validation of Anthroposophy."

** Please see page 155 for Dessoir's response to this essay.

III

Franz Brentano

In Memoriam

For the reasons expressed in the previous chapter, it is impossible to speak adequately about the relation between anthropology (natural science) and anthroposophy (spiritual science) in connection with Max Dessoir's book *Beyond the Soul*. But I believe that this relation can become visible if I place here what I wrote with a different intention, in memory, namely, of the philosopher Franz Brentano, who died in Zurich in March 1917. The departure of this man, whom I held in the highest esteem, had the effect of bringing before my soul anew his significant life's work; it moved me to express the following.

At this moment when the death of this revered person has interrupted his work, it seems to me that I might make an attempt, from an anthroposophical viewpoint to arrive at a view of Franz Brentano's philosophical life's work. I believe that the anthroposophical viewpoint will not let me fall into a one-sided evaluation of Brentano's world view. I assume this for two reasons. Firstly, no one can accuse Brentano's way of picturing things of having even the slightest tendency in an anthroposophical direction. If he himself had had any cause to judge it, he would certainly have rejected it decisively. Secondly, from my anthroposophical viewpoint, I am in a position to approach the philosophy of Franz Brentano with unconditional reverence.

With respect to my first reason, I believe I am correct in saying that if he had arrived at an assessment of what I mean by anthroposophy, Brentano would have shaped it the way he did his judgment on Plotinus' philosophy. As with it he would certainly also have said of anthroposophy: "mystical darkness and an uncontrolled fantasy roving into unknown regions." As with neo-platonism he would have urged caution with respect to anthroposophy "so as not, enticed by empty appearances, to lose oneself in the labyrinthine passages of a pseudophilosophy." Yes, he may also have found anthroposophy's way of thinking to be too dilettantish even to be worthy of being reckoned to the philosophies which he judged the way he did those of Fichte, Schelling, and Hegel. In his inaugural Vienna address he said of them: "Perhaps the recent past has also been an ... epoch of decay, in which all concepts ran together in a muddy way, and no trace was to be found of a method in keeping with facts." I believe that Brentano would have judged in this way, even though I also of course not only consider this judgment to be totally unfounded, but also regard as unjustified any pairing of anthroposophy with the philosophies with which Brentano would probably have paired it.

Now with respect to my other reason for coming to terms with Brentano's philosophy, I must confess that for me his philosophy belongs to the most inviting accomplishments in soul research in modern times. It is true that I was only able to hear a few of Brentano's lectures in Vienna some thirty-six years ago; but from then on I have followed his literary activity with warmest interest. Unfortunately, when measured against my wish to hear from him, his publications came at too great an interval from each other. And these writings are mostly of such a kind that one peered through them as though through little openings into a room filled with treasures; one looked, so to speak, through occasional publications upon a broad realm of the unpublished thoughts that this exceptional man bore within himself—bore within himself in such a way that it strove in continuous evolution toward lofty goals of knowledge. When, therefore, in 1911, after a long interval there appeared his book on *Aristotle*, his brilliant book *Aristotle's Teaching on the Origin of the Human Spirit*, and his republishing of the most important sections of his *Psychology*, with its penetrating addenda, the reading of these books was a series of festive joys for me.

With respect to Franz Brentano I feel myself imbued with a kind of soul disposition of which I believe I may say that one acquires it when the anthroposophical viewpoint—out of scientifically acquired conviction—in fact takes hold of one's soul disposition. I strive to gain insight into the value of his views, even though I am under no illusion about the fact that he could—yes, would even have had to—think about anthroposophy in the way indicated above. I am truly not saying this here in order to fall foolishly into a vain self-critique of my soul disposition when confronted by hostile or differing views, but rather because I know how many misunderstandings of my assessments of other spiritual streams have occurred through the fact that in my books I have so often expressed myself in a way stemming from this soul disposition. It seems to me that the whole methodology of Brentano's soul research is permeated with the basic thoughts that moved him in 1868 to set up his guiding principle. As he was entering his philosophical professorship at that time in Würzburg, he placed his way of picturing things into the light of the thesis: True philosophical research cannot be of any other kind than that which is considered valid in natural-scientific cognition. "Vera phi-

losophiae methodus nulla alia nisi scientiae naturalis est."[*]
When he then published the first volume of his *Psychology
from an Empirical Standpoint* in 1874—at the time of entering
his Vienna professorship—he sought to present soul phenomena scientifically, in accordance with the above guiding
principle. What Brentano wanted to accomplish with this
book and its further manifestations in publications during
his lifetime pose a significant scientific problem for me. As
is clear from his book, Brentano counted on a series of books
to contain his psychology. He promised to publish a second
book shortly after the first. But no sequel was ever published to his first book, which contained only the preliminary
ideas of his psychology. When he published the lecture he
had given in 1889 to the Vienna Bar Association, entitled *The
Origins of Moral Knowledge,* he wrote in the preface:

> It would be a mistake, just because of the chance
> request for this lecture to regard it as the passing
> work of the moment. It offers the fruits of years of
> reflection. Of everything I have published so far its
> contents are definitely the ripest creation. They be-
> long to the thought complex of a "descriptive psy-
> chology" which I dare to hope I will be able to reveal
> in its full scope to the public in the not too distant
> future. Its far removal from any tradition and more
> especially the significant development of my own
> views as presented in *Psychology from an Empirical
> Standpoint* will clearly show that I have not in fact
> been idle during my long literary retirement.

---

[*] He later spoke about his setting up of this thesis in the lecture he held in the
Vienna Philosophical Society in 1892 (published under the title *The Future of
Philosophy*). What I refer to as Brentano's later reference to his thesis is on
page 3.

66

But this "descriptive psychology" also never appeared. By reading his *Research into the Psychology of the Senses* (1907), which is restricted to one small area, devotees of Brentano's philosophy can reckon what they would have gained from such a descriptive psychology.

The question must be asked: What made Brentano hold back ever and again from continuing his publications, and then not to publish at all something he believed would be ready shortly? I confess that I was shaken to the core when I read the following words in the memorial to Brentano written by Alois Höfler in May 1917: "Brentano was working ahead so confidently on his main problem, proof of God's existence, that a few years ago an excellent Viennese doctor and close friend of Brentano's told me that Brentano had assured him a short while ago that he would now have his proof of God's existence ready in a few weeks ...." I felt the same way when I read in another memorial (by Utitz): "The work that he loved the most fervently, that he applied himself to his whole life long, remains unpublished."

It seems to me that Brentano's destiny with respect to his projected publications represents a weighty, spiritual-scientific problem. It is true that we can approach this problem only if we are willing to study, in its own special character, what Brentano was able to communicate to the world. I consider it important to note that Brentano wants, with real acumen, to establish as a basis for his psychological research a pure mental picture of the genuine soul element. He asks himself: What is characteristic of all the occurrences that one must address as soulful? And he found what he expressed in the following way in the addenda of his *Psychology* (1911): "What is characteristic of every soul activity consists, as I believe I have shown, in its relation to

67

something as object." Mental picturing is a soul activity. Characteristic of it is that I not only picture but that I picture *something*, that my mental picture relates to something. Borrowing from medieval philosophy, Brentano calls this characteristic of soul phenomena an "intentional relation." In another place he said:

> The characteristic common to everything of a soul nature is what is often called "consciousness,"—to use a term that unfortunately can be quite misleading—i.e., it is a subjective activity, in a so-called *intentional* relation to something that perhaps is not real but nevertheless is given in an inwardly objective way. No hearing without something heard; no believing without something believed; no hoping without something hoped for; no striving without something striven for; no joy without something to be joyous about; and so on.

This intentional inner awareness, therefore, is something which in fact guides us as a kind of leitmotiv in such a way that through it one recognizes everything to which we can apply it as being of a soul nature.

Brentano contrasts soul phenomena with physical phenomena: colors, sound, space, and many others. He finds that these last are different from the soul phenomena through the fact that an intentional relation is not characteristic of them. And he limits himself to attributing this relation to soul phenomena and to denying it to physical phenomena. But now, precisely when one learns to know Brentano's view on the intentional relation, our inner vision is led to the question: Does not a viewpoint like this require us to look at physical phenomena also from the same viewpoint? Now someone who, in the sense of Brentano, tests physical phenomena for a common element as he did with soul phenomena will find that every phenomenon in the physical realm exists *through (by virtue of) something else.* When a body dissolves in a fluid, this phenomenon of the dissolved body occurs through the relation to it of the dissolving fluid. When phosphorus changes color under the influence of the sun, this phenomenon points in the same direction. All the qualities of the physical world exist through the interrelations of things to each other. What Moleschott says is correct for physical existence: "All existence is an existence through qualities. But there is no quality that does not exist through a relation." Just as everything of a soul nature contains something *in itself* by which it points to something *outside* itself, so conversely, a physical thing is so constituted that it is what it is through the relation to it of something outer. Someone like Brentano who emphasizes with so much acumen the intentional relation of everything of a soul nature, must he not also direct his attention upon a characteristic element of physical phenomena that results from the same train of thought? At the very least, it seems certain that a study like this of the soul element can discover the relation of this soul element to the physical world only if it takes this characteristic element into consideration.[*]

Now Brentano discovers three kinds of intentional relations in our soul life. The first is the *mental picturing* of something; the second is the acceptance or rejection that expresses itself in judging; the third is the loving or hating that is experienced in our *feeling.* If I say, "God is just," I am picturing something to myself; but I do not yet accept or

---

[*] Please see the last part of addendum 7, "Brentano's Separation of the Soul from What Is External to the Soul," which begins on page 144.

reject what I am picturing; but if I say, "There is a God," I accept what I am picturing through a *judgment*. If I say, "I like to feel pleasure," I am not only judging, I am experiencing a *feeling*. From such presuppositions Brentano distinguishes three basic categories of soul experiences: mental picturing, judging, and feeling (or the phenomena of loving and hating). He replaces the usual division of soul phenomena (into mental picturing, feeling, and willing) with these three basic categories. So whereas many people put mental picturing and judging into the same category, Brentano separates them. He does not agree with combining them, because, unlike other thinkers, he does not regard judgments as merely the connecting of mental pictures, but rather, in fact, as the acceptance or rejection of what has been pictured, which are not activities of mere mental picturing. On the other hand, with respect to their soul content, feeling and will, which other people separate, merge for Brentano into one. What is experienced in the soul when one feels oneself drawn to do something, or repelled from doing it, is the same as what one experiences when one is drawn to pleasure or repelled by pain.

It is evident from Brentano's writing that he sets great store in having replaced the traditional division of soul experience into thinking, feeling, and willing by the other one into mental picturing, judging, and loving/hating. By this division he seeks to clear the way for an understanding of what truth is, on the one hand, and moral goodness on the other. For him truth is based on right judgment; moral goodness on right love. He finds that "We call something true when its acceptance is right. We call something good when the love we bring to it is right."

One can see from Brentano's presentations that when he observes the right acceptance in judgment with respect to truth and the right experience of love with respect to moral goodness, he is taking a sharp look at soul phenomena and circumscribing them. But, within his thought sphere, one can find nothing that would suffice to make the transition from our soul experience of mental picturing to that of judging. No matter where we look in Brentano's thought sphere we seek in vain the answer to the question: What is happening when the soul is conscious of not merely picturing something to itself, but also of finding itself moved to accept this something though judgment?

Just as little can one escape a question with respect to our right love of the morally good. Within the region that Brentano circumscribes as the "soul element," the only phenomenon pertaining to moral action is right loving. But does not a relation to the outer world also belong to a moral action? With respect to a characterization of a deed for the world, is it enough to say: It is a deed that is rightly loved?[*]

In following Brentano's trains of thought, we mainly have a feeling that they are always fruitful because they take up a problem and move it in one direction with acumen and scientific thoroughness; but one also feels that Brentano's trains of thought do not reach the goal that his starting points promise us. Such a feeling can come over us when we compare his threefold division of our soul life into mental picturing, judging, and loving/hating to the other division into mental picturing, feeling, and willing. One follows his views with a certain amount of agreement, but ultimately

---

[*] Please see addendum 5 on page 125: "The Real Basis of an Intentional Relation."

remains unconvinced that he has done sufficient justice to the reasons for membering the soul the other way. Let us just take the example of the conclusions he draws from his soul division about the true, the beautiful, and the good. Whoever members our soul life into cognitional mental picturing, feeling, and willing can hardly do otherwise than closely connect our striving for truth with mental picturing, our experience of beauty with feeling, and our accomplishment of the good with willing. The matter looks different in the light of Brentano's thought. There the mental pictures as such have no relation to each other by which the truth as such could already reveal itself. When the soul is striving to perfect itself relative to its mental pictures, its ideal cannot therefore be the truth; beauty is its ideal. Truth does not lie on the path of mere mental picturing; it lies on the path of judging. And the morally good does not find itself as essentially united with our willing; it is a content of our feeling; for, to love rightly is a feeling experience. For our ordinary consciousness, however, the truth can be sought, after all, in our mentally picturing cognition. For, even though the judgment that leads to the truth does not lie only in the connecting of mental pictures but rather is based on an acceptance or rejection of the mental pictures, still the acceptance or rejection of these pictures can only be experienced by our consciousness in mental pictures.

And even though the mental pictures in which something beautiful presents itself to the soul do manifest in certain relationships within our life of mental pictures, still, the beauty is *experienced*, after all, by our feeling.

And although something morally good should call forth the right love in our soul, still the essential factor in the morally good after all, is the *accomplishment* through the will of what is rightly loved.

One only recognizes what we actually have in Brentano's thoughts about the threefold division of our soul life when one realizes that he is speaking of something completely different from what those thinkers mean who divide it into mental picturing, feeling, and willing. The latter simply want to describe the experiences of ordinary consciousness. And this consciousness experiences itself in the different kinds of activity of mental picturing, feeling, and willing. What does one actually experience there? I tried to answer this question in my book *The Riddle of Man*[*] and summarized the findings presented there in the following words:

> Human soul experience, as it manifests in thinking, feeling, and willing, is at first bound to the bodily instruments. And this experience takes shape in ways determined by these instruments. If someone asserts, however, that when he observes the manifestations of the soul through the body he is seeing the *real life* of the soul, he is then caught up in the same error as someone who believes that *his actual form* is brought forth by the mirror in front of him just because the mirror possesses the necessary prerequisites through which his *image* appears. Within certain limits this image, as image, is indeed dependent upon the form of the mirror, etc.; but *what this image represents* has nothing to do with the mirror. In order to completely fulfill its essential being within the sense world, human soul life must have an *image* of its being. It must have its image in

---

[*] Published by Mercury Press, 1990. See pages 132f. Ed.

consciousness; otherwise it would indeed have an existence, but no picture, no knowledge of it. This *image*, now, that lives in the ordinary consciousness of the soul is fully determined by the bodily instruments. Without these, the image would not be there, just as the mirror image would not be there without the mirror. *But what appears through this image*, the soul element itself, is—in its essential being—no more dependent upon the bodily instrument than the person standing before the mirror is dependent upon the mirror. The soul is not dependent upon the bodily instruments; only the ordinary consciousness of the soul is so.[*]

If one is describing the realm of consciousness that is dependent upon our bodily organization, one is correct in membering it into mental picturing, feeling, and willing.[**] But Brentano is describing something different. Bear in mind to begin with that by "judging," he means an acceptance or rejection of a content of mental pictures. Our judgment is active within our life of mental pictures; but it does not simply accept the mental pictures that arise in the soul; through acceptance or rejection it relates them to a reality. If one observes more closely, this relating of our mental pictures to a reality can only be found in a soul activity that occurs within the soul itself. But this can never totally correspond to what the soul produces when, through judging, it

---

[*] Although the following comment is superfluous, I am sure, to many readers, I would still like to add that, by the very nature of the matter, with my comparison of consciousness to a mirror image, I am not referring to the usual practice of calling our world of mental pictures a mirror image of the outer world; I am calling the soul's experiences in ordinary consciousness a mirror image of the genuine soul element.

[**] Please see addendum 6 on page 131: "The Physical and Spiritual Dependencies of Man's Being."

relates a mental picture to a sense perception. For there the compulsion of the outer impression holds sway, which is not experienced in a purely inner way, but only as an echoed experience, and as a mentally pictured, *echoed experience* leads to its acceptance or rejection. On the other hand, what Brentano describes corresponds totally in this respect with the kind of cognition that we called "Imaginative cognition" in the first essay of this book. In Imaginative cognition the mental picturing of our ordinary consciousness is not simply accepted; it is developed further in inner soul experience so that out of it the power emerges to relate the soul's experiences to a *spiritual* reality in such a way that this reality is accepted or rejected. Brentano's concept of judgment, therefore, is not perfectly realized in our ordinary consciousness, but only in the soul that is active in Imaginative cognition.

Furthermore, it is clear that, through Brentano's complete separation of the concept of mental picturing from the concept of judgment, he takes mental picturing to be mere *image*. But this is how ordinary mental picturing lives in Imaginative cognition. So even this second quality that anthroposophy attributes to Imaginative cognition is to be found in Brentano's characterization of soul phenomena.

What is more, Brentano addresses the experiences of feeling as manifestations of love and hate. Whoever ascends to Imaginative cognition must, in fact, for supersensible vision, transform the kind of soul experience that manifests in ordinary consciousness as loving and hating—in Brentano's sense of the words—in such a way that we can confront certain characteristics of spiritual reality that are described in my book *Theosophy*, for example, in the following way:

Among the first things one must acquire for an orientation in the soul world is the ability to distinguish between its different kinds of entities in the same way that one distinguishes in the physical world between solid, fluid, and gaseous entities. To attain this, one must know the two basic forces that are of primary significance here. One can call them "sympathy" and "antipathy." The way these basic forces work in a soul entity determines its kind.

Whereas loving and hating remain something subjective for the life of the soul in the sense world, Imaginative cognition lives along with objective occurrences in the soul world through inner experiences that are equivalent to loving and hating. There also, where he is speaking about soul phenomena, Brentano describes a characteristic of Imaginative cognition through which this cognition already extends into the realm of a still higher kind of knowledge* and from the fact that he presents moral goodness as right loving one can see that he has a mental picture of an *objective* kind of loving and hating in contrast to ordinary consciousness' subjective kind of feeling.

Finally, one must pay particular attention to the fact that for Brentano willing is absent from the realm of soul phenomena. Now, the willing that flows out of ordinary consciousness belongs entirely to the physical world. Although *in itself* it is a purely spiritual being manifesting in the physical world, our willing, in the form in which it can be

---

* The first form of a "seeing cognition"—Imaginative cognition—passes over into the second form, which is called "Inspired cognition" in my books. In addendum 6 on page 131, "The Physical and Spiritual Dependencies of Man's Being," there is a description of how an Imagination that has already passed over into Inspiration actually lives in Brentano's definition of loving and hating.

thought by ordinary consciousness, realizes itself totally in the physical world. If one is describing the ordinary consciousness present in the physical world, willing must not be absent from this picture. If one is describing the seeing consciousness, nothing from our mental pictures about ordinary willing must pass over into these descriptions. For, in the soul world to which Imaginative consciousness is related, what happens as the result of a soul impulse is different from what occurs through the acts of will characteristic of the physical world. So when Brentano focuses on the soul phenomena in *that* realm in which Imaginative cognition is active, the concept of willing must evaporate for him.

It really seems obvious that, in describing the essential being of soul phenomena, Brentano was actually compelled to depict the essential being of seeing cognition. This is clear even from certain details of his descriptions. Let us look at one example from the many that could be introduced. He says: "The characteristic common to everything of a soul nature is what is often called 'consciousness'—to use a term that unfortunately can be quite misleading...." But, when one is only describing those soul phenomena which by belonging to ordinary consciousness are determined by the bodily organization, this term is not at all misleading. Brentano has a sense for the fact, however, that the real soul does not live in this ordinary consciousness, and he feels impelled to speak about the essential being of this real soul in pictures that, to be sure, must be misleading if one wants to apply the usual concept of consciousness to them.

Brentano proceeds in his investigations in such a way that he pursues the phenomena of the anthropological realm up to that point where they compel an unbiased person to form pictures of the soul that coincide with what anthroposophy, following its own paths, discovers about the soul. And the findings on both paths prove to be in fullest harmony with each other, precisely through Brentano's psychology. Brentano himself, however, did not wish to abandon the anthropological path. He was hindered from doing this by his interpretations of the guiding principle he had set up for himself: "True philosophical research cannot be of any other kind than that considered valid by the natural-scientific kind of cognition." A different interpretation of this guiding principle could have led him to recognize that the natural-scientific approach is seen in the right light precisely at the point when one becomes aware that this approach, in accordance with its own essential nature, must transform itself in dealing with this spiritual realm. Brentano never wished to make the true soul phenomena—which he called soul phenomena "as such"—into objects of an avowed consciousness. If he had done this, he would have progressed from anthropology to anthroposophy. He feared this path, because he was only able to regard it as an erring into "mystical darkness and an uncontrolled roving of fantasy into unknown regions." He would not permit himself to investigate at all what his own psychological view demanded. Every time he was faced with the necessity of extending his own path into the anthroposophical realm he stopped short. He wished to answer by anthropology the questions that can only be answered by anthroposophy. This effort was doomed to failure. Because it had to fail, he could not proceed in a satisfying way to develop further what he had begun. To judge by the findings in the first volume of his *Psychology from an Empirical Standpoint*, if he had continued on with it, it would have to have become anthroposophy. If he really had produced his *Descriptive Psychology*, anthroposophy would have to have shone through it everywhere. If he had carried further the ethics in his book *The Origins of Moral Knowledge*—in a way corresponding to its starting point—he would have to have hit upon anthroposophy.

Before Brentano's soul there stood the possibility of a psychology that could not be given a purely anthropological form. Anthropology cannot even think at all about the most significant questions that must be raised about human soul life. Modern psychology only wants to be anthropological because it considers anything going beyond it to be unscientific. Brentano says, however:

> The laws of mental association, of the development of convictions and opinions, and of the germinating of pleasure and love, all these would be anything but a true compensation for not gaining certainty about the hopes of a Plato and Aristotle for the continued existence of our better part after the dissolution of the body.... And if the difference between these two views really did signify the inclusion or exclusion of the question of immortality, this would have to be called an extremely portentous difference, and a metaphysical investigation of substance as the bearer of [soul] states would be unavoidable.

Anthroposophy shows that metaphysical speculation cannot take one into the region indicated by Brentano; the only way to enter it is through activation of soul powers which cannot descend into ordinary consciousness. Through the fact that in his philosophy Brentano portrays the essential being of the soul in such a way that the essential being of seeing cognition comes to clear expression in this portrayal, this philosophy is a perfect vindication of anthroposophy. And one can regard Brentano as a philosophical investigator whose path takes him to the very doors of anthroposophy, but does not *wish* to open these doors, because the picture he has made for himself of natural-scientific thinking created the belief in him that by opening these doors he would land himself in the abyss of nonscience.

* * *

The difficulties often confronting Brentano when he wishes to extend his picture of the soul stem from the fact that he relates his picture of the essential being of the soul element to what is present in ordinary consciousness. He is motivated to do this by his wish to remain in the thought mode that seems to him to be scientifically valid. But this approach, with its means of cognition, can only in fact attain to that part of the soul element that is present as the content of ordinary consciousness. This content, however, is not the real soul element but only its mirror image. Brentano grasps this image only from the side of intelligent understanding, and not from the other side, the side of observation. In his concepts he paints a picture of the soul phenomena that occur in the reality of the soul; when he observes, he believes himself to have a reality in his mirror image of the soul element.[*]

Another philosophical stream that Brentano met with the strongest antipathy—that of Eduard von Hartmann—also took its start from a natural-scientific way of picturing

---

[*] Please see addendum 7, on page 145, "Brentano's Separation of the Soul Element from What is External to the Soul."

the world. Eduard von Hartmann has recognized the image character of ordinary consciousness. But he also utterly rejects any possibility of bringing its corresponding reality into human consciousness in any way. He consigns this reality to the region of the unconscious. He grants the power to speak about this region only to the hypothetical application of the concepts which one has formed through ordinary consciousness and extended beyond it.* Anthroposophy maintains that spiritual observation can go beyond the realm of ordinary consciousness. And that concepts are also accessible to this spiritual observation that no more need to be merely hypothetical than those acquired in the sense-perceptible world.

For Eduard von Hartmann the supersensible world is not known directly; it is inferred from what we know directly. Hartmann belongs to those present-day philosophers who do not wish to form concepts without having, as a starting point for forming these concepts, the testimony of sense observation and of their experiences in ordinary consciousness. Brentano forms such concepts, however. But he is mistaken about the reality in which they can be formed through observation. His spirit proves to be curiously divided. He would like to be a pure natural scientist, thinking in the natural-scientific mode that has developed in recent times. And yet he must form concepts that this mode would only consider justified if one did not consider this mode to be the only valid one. This division in Brentano's investigative spirit can be explained if one really studies his first books: *The Manifold Significance of "Being," According to Aris-*

* This view is expressed in his two books *Modern Psychology*, Leipzig 1901, and *Outline of Psychology*, Bad Sachsa 1908.

81

totle (1862), *The Psychology of Aristotle* (1867), and *The Creationism of Aristotle* (1882).

In these books Brentano follows Aristotle's trains of thought with exemplary scholarship. And in this pursuit he acquires a kind of thinking that cannot be limited to the concepts that hold sway in anthropology. In these books he has in view a concept of soul that derives the soul element out of the spiritual element. This soul element, stemming from the spiritual element, uses the organism—formed by physical processes—to form mental pictures for itself within sense-perceptible existence. What forms mental pictures for itself in the soul is spiritual in nature; it is Aristotle's "nous." But this "nous" is a twofold being; as "nous pathetikos," it only suffers things to happen to it; it allows itself to be stimulated to its mental pictures by the impressions given it by the organism. In order for these mental pictures to appear as they are in the active soul, however, this activity must work as "nous poetikos." What the "nous pathetikos" provides would be mere phenomena within a dark soul existence; they are illuminated by the "nous poetikos." Brentano says in this connection: "The 'nous poetikos' is the light that illumines the phantasms and makes visible to our spiritual eye the spiritual within the sense-perceptible." If one wants to understand Brentano, the point is not only how far he went in taking up Aristotle's mental pictures into his own convictions, but above all that he moved about in these pictures with his own thinking in a devoted way. In doing so, however, his thinking was active in a realm in which the starting point of sensory observation—and along with it the anthropological basis for forming concepts—is not present. And this basic characteristic of his thinking remained in Brentano's research. True, he

82

wants to grant validity only to what can be recognized as conforming with the present-day, natural-scientific mode; but he has to form thoughts that do not belong in that realm. Now, according to the purely natural-scientific method, one can only say something about soul phenomena insofar as they are mirror images—determined by the bodily organization—of the real being of the soul; i.e., insofar as, in their nature as mirror images, they arise and pass away with the bodily organization. What Brentano must think the reality of the soul to be, however, is something spiritual, something independent of the bodily organization, in fact, that through the "nous poetikos" makes visible to our spiritual eye the spiritual within the sense-perceptible.

The fact that Brentano can move about with his thinking in such realms prohibits him from conceiving of the soul's essential being as something arising through the bodily organization and passing away with it. Because he rejects supersensible observation, however, he can observe within the soul's essential being no content that extends beyond physical existence. The moment he tries to ascribe a content to the soul that the soul could unfold without the help of the bodily organization, Brentano feels himself to be in a world for which he finds no mental pictures. In this frame of mind he turns to Aristotle and finds there also a picture of the soul that gives him no content other than that acquired in bodily existence. Characteristic in its one-sidedness is something Brentano wrote in this connection in his *Psychology of Aristotle:*

> Now just as a person, when he has lost a foot or another limb, is no longer a complete substance, so, when his whole bodily part has fallen prey to death, he is of course much less a complete substance. To

be sure, the spiritual part continues to exist; but *those are very much in error* who, like Plato, believe that the separation from the body is a benefit to them and, as it were, a liberation from an oppressive prison; the soul, after all, must now renounce all the numerous services that the bodily forces have rendered.

Brentano got into an extraordinarily interesting dispute with the philosopher Eduard Zeller over Aristotle's conception of the essential being of the soul. Zeller maintained that it is in line with Aristotle's views to accept a pre-existence of the soul before its union with the bodily organization, whereas Brentano denied any such view to Aristotle, and only allowed Aristotle to think that the soul is first created into the bodily organization; so the soul has no pre-existence, but does indeed have an after-existence when the body disintegrates. Brentano maintained that only Plato accepted pre-existence, but Aristotle did not. It is undeniable that the reasons Brentano brings for his opinion and against Zeller's are weighty ones. Irrespective of Brentano's intelligent interpretation of Aristotle's relevant assertions, we are indeed faced with a difficulty in ascribing to Aristotle a belief in the pre-existence of the soul when we consider that any such belief seems to contradict a basic principle of Aristotelian metaphysics. Aristotle states, namely, that a "form" could never exist before the "substance" that bears the form. A spherical shape never exists without the substance that fills it. Since Aristotle considers the soul element to be the "form" of the bodily organization, however, it seems that we cannot ascribe to him the belief that the soul could exist before the bodily organization arose.

Now Brentano, with his concept of the soul, became so caught up in the Aristotelian picture of the impossibility of pre-existence that he could not see how this picture breaks down at a crucial point. Can one really think of "form" and "matter" in such a way that one accepts the view that form could not exist prior to the matter that fills it? The spherical shape could not after all be present prior to the substance filling it? The sphere, as it appears in a substance, is certainly not present prior to the balling up of the substance. *Before* the substance comes together like this, however, those forces are present which act upon this substance and whose effect upon the substance reveals itself in its spherical shape. And within these forces, prior to the appearing of this spherical shape, this shape is certainly living already in *another* way.* Had Brentano not felt bound, through his interpretation of the natural-scientific approach, to find the content for his concept of the soul from observation of the bodily organization, he would perhaps have noticed that the Aristotelian concept of the soul is itself burdened with an inner contradiction. Thus, through his study of Aristotle's world view, he could only think up pictures of the soul that lift it out of the realm of the bodily organization, but without indicating a soul content that allows me, with

---

* A mistaken view about the validity of the assertion that form cannot exist prior to the matter filling it can arise in connection with crystal formation only because there the form seems to emerge directly out of the forces dwelling in the matter. Nevertheless, unbiased thinking cannot do otherwise than situate the formative forces within the material element *before* the formed matter actually arises. Aristotle's picture becomes completely untenable, however, when we consider the plant, whose *formative* forces can certainly not be sought in the conditions within the seed alone, but rather in the effects of the outer world that are present long before the formation of the sense-perceptible plant.

85

unbiased thinking, to be able to really picture the soul as independent of the bodily organization.

Besides Aristotle, Leibnitz is another philosopher whom Brentano particularly appreciates. It is especially Leibnitz's way of viewing the soul that seems to have attracted him. Now one can say that Leibnitz has a way of picturing things in this realm that seems to be a significant extension of Aristotle's view. Whereas, Aristotle makes the essential content of human thinking dependent upon sense observation, Leibnitz frees this content from its sensory foundation. Following Aristotle one will accept the statement: There is nothing in thinking that was not previously in the senses (*nihil est in intellectu, quod non fuerit in sensu*); Leibnitz, however, is of the view that there is nothing in thinking that was not previously in the senses, *except* thinking itself (*nihil est in intellectu, quod non fuerit in sensu, nisi ipse intellectus*). It would be incorrect to ascribe to Aristotle the view that the essential being active in thinking is the result of forces working in the body. However, by making the "nous pathetikos" the passive receiver of sense impressions and the "nous poetikos" the illuminator of these impressions, nothing remained in his philosophy that could become the *content* of a soul life independent of sensory existence. In this respect, Leibnitz's statement proves to be more fruitful. Through it our attention is especially directed toward the essential being of the soul that is independent of the bodily organization. This attention, to be sure, is limited to the merely intellectual part of this essential being. And in this regard, Leibnitz's statement is one-sided. Nevertheless, this statement is a guideline that in our present-day natural-scientific age can lead to something that Leibnitz could not yet attain. In his time our picture of the purely natural origin of the characteristics of the bodily organization was still too imperfect. This is different now. To a certain extent today one can know scientifically how the organic bodily forces are inherited from one's ancestors, and how the soul operates within these inherited organic forces. To be sure, many who believe that they are taking the correct "natural-scientific standpoint" will not acknowledge the following view, even though, for a correct grasp of natural-scientific knowledge, it proves necessary: that everything by which the soul operates in the physical body is determined by the bodily forces that proceed from ancestor to descendant in a line of physical inheritance, *with the exception* of the soul content itself. This is how we can extend Leibnitz's statement today. And then it represents the anthropological validation of the anthroposophical way of looking at things. Then it directs the soul to seek its own essential content within a spiritual world, and to do this in fact through a different kind of cognition than that customary in anthropology. For, anthropology has access only to what is experienced by the bodily organization in ordinary consciousness.[*]

The view is quite tenable that Brentano had all the prerequisites, with Leibnitz as his starting point, for opening our vision to the essential being of the soul as an entity

---

[*] There are thinkers who are repelled by the view that the essential kernel of one's soul is not inherited from its physical ancestors but originates from the spiritual world, because this view demeans the process of human procreation. The philosopher J. Frohschammer is one of these thinkers (see his book *The Origin of Human Souls*). According to him, we must believe that even children's souls stem from their parents, since "these living human beings do not beget mere bodies or animals" (see also Frohschammer's book on *The Philosophy of Thomas Aquinas*). An objection based on this opinion does not apply to the view we are presenting in this book. For, one need not think that the soul kernel, descending from the spiritual world and uniting itself with what is inherited from the ancestors, is unconnected with the souls of its parents before birth, even though one does not picture this soul kernel as arising *through* the act of procreation.

anchored in the spirit, and for strengthening the results of this vision through today's natural-scientific knowledge. Anyone who pursues Brentano's presentations can see the path laid out before him. The path that leads to a purely spiritual, recognizable soul being, could have become visible to him, if he had developed further what already lay in the sphere of his awareness when he wrote such statements as these:

> But how are we to picture the engagement of the Godhead in the appearance of a human soul in a body? After creatively bringing forth the spiritual part of man out of all eternity, did the Godhead then connect it with an embryo in such a way that this spiritual part—existing up till then as a distinct spiritual substance unto itself—now ceased to be a real entity unto itself and became a part of a human nature, or did the Godhead only then bring forth this spiritual part creatively? When Aristotle accepted the first possibility, he had to believe that the same spirit would be connected again and again with ever different embryos; for, according to him, the human race perpetuates itself by endless procreation, while on the other hand, the number of spirits existing through all eternity can only be a limited one. All Aristotle interpreters agree, however, that he rejected palingenesis* in his more mature period. Therefore, this possibility is out of the question. (see his book *Aristotle and his World View*, 1911)

* Literally, "rebirth." Ed.

Although the validation of a spiritual vision of the soul's repeated earth lives through palingenesis does not lie in Aristotle's train of thought, it could have resulted for Brentano through his connecting his soul concept, which he had refined through his work with Aristotle, with the knowledge of modern natural science.

Brentano's receptivity to the epistemology of medieval philosophy would have made it all the easier for him to have taken this path. Anyone who really grasps this epistemology acquires a number of ideas able to relate the results of modern natural science to the spiritual world in a way that is not visible to the ideas arising in the purely natural-scientific research of anthropology. In many circles today one fails to recognize how much a way of picturing things like that of Thomas Aquinas can deepen natural science in a spiritual direction. In such circles one believes that modern natural-scientific knowledge requires a turning away from that way of picturing things. The truth is that one wishes at first to encompass what natural science recognizes as the being of the world with thoughts that, upon closer inspection, turn out to be incomplete in themselves. Their completion would consist in our considering them to be the kind of essential entities in the soul that they are thought to be in Thomas Aquinas' way of picturing things. And Brentano did find himself on his way to gaining the right relation to this way of picturing things. He writes, after all:

> In writing *The Manifold Significance of Being According to Aristotle* and later my *Psychology of Aristotle*, I wished to further our understanding of his teachings in a twofold way: first and foremost, directly through an illumination of several of the most important points of his teachings; then secondly

and indirectly—but in a more general way—by opening new and helpful sources of understanding. I drew the reader's attention to the incisive commentaries of Thomas Aquinas and showed that one can find in them truer presentations of many of Aristotle's teachings than are to be found in later interpretations.*

Brentano barred the path that such studies could have revealed to him, because of his inclination toward Bacon's and Locke's way of picturing things and toward everything philosophically connected with that approach. He regarded that approach above all as according with the natural-scientific method. Precisely this approach, however, leads one to think that the content of our soul life is utterly dependent upon the sense world. And since this way of thinking wants to proceed only anthropologically, only *that* enters into its domain as psychological results which, in truth, is not a soul reality, but only a mirror image of this reality, i.e., the content of ordinary consciousness.

If Brentano had recognized the image nature of ordinary consciousness, he would not have been able, in his pursuit of anthropological research, to stop short at the gates leading into anthroposophy.

One could of course counter my view with the opinion that Brentano simply lacked the gift of spiritual vision and so did not seek the transition from anthropology to anthroposophy, even though he was moved by his own particular spiritual disposition to characterize soul phenomena in an interesting form and so intelligently that this form can be validated through anthroposophy. I myself am not of this

* See Brentano's *Aristotle's Teachings on the Origins of the Human Spirit*, 1911.

90

opinion, however. I am not of the view that spiritual vision is attainable only as a special gift of exceptional personalities. I must regard this vision as a faculty of the human soul that anyone can acquire for himself if he awakens in himself the soul experiences that lead to it. And Brentano's nature seems to me to be quite especially capable of such an awakening. I believe, however, that one can hinder such an awakening with theories that oppose it; that one keeps this vision from arising if one is entangled in ideas that from the beginning call into question the validity of such vision. And Brentano kept this vision from arising in his soul through the fact that for him the ideas that so beautifully validate this vision always succumbed to the ideas that reject it and that make one fear that through such vision one could "lose oneself in the labyrinthine passages of a pseudophilosophy."[*]

* * *

In 1895 Brentano published a reprint of a lecture he had given in the Literary Society in Vienna with reference to a book by H. Lorm, *Baseless Optimism*. This lecture contains his view about the "four phases of philosophy and their present status." There Brentano expresses his belief that the course of development of philosophical research can be compared, in a certain respect, with the history of the arts.

> Whereas other sciences, as long as they are practiced at all, show a continuous progress interrupted only occasionally by periods of inaction, philosophy, like the arts, shows decadent periods, in addition to those of positive development, that are often

---

[*] Please see addendum 8 on page 151, "An Objection Often Raised against Anthroposophy."

no less rich—yes, even richer—in epoch-making occurrences than periods of healthy fruitfulness.

Brentano distinguishes three such periods in the course
of philosophy's development where healthy fruitfulness
has passed over into decadence. Each of these periods begins with the fact that out of a purely philosophical
astonishment over the riddles of the world, a truly scientific
interest stirs and that this interest then seeks knowledge out
of a genuine, pure drive to know. This healthy epoch is then
followed by another in which the first stage of decadence
appears. The purely scientific interest recedes, and people
look for thoughts by which to regulate their social and
personal lives, and to find their way among them. There,
philosophy no longer wishes to serve a pure striving for
knowledge, but rather the interests of life. A further decline
occurs in the third period. Through the uncertainty of
thoughts that did not arise out of purely scientific interests,
one loses confidence in the possibility of true knowledge
and falls into skepticism. The fourth epoch is one of complete decay. In the third epoch, doubt had undermined the
whole scientific foundation of philosophy. Out of unscientific dark depths one seeks to arrive at the truth through
mystical experience in fantastical, blurred concepts. Brentano pictured the first cycle of development as beginning
with Greek natural philosophy; according to him, this
healthy phase ended with Aristotle. Within this phase he
holds Anaxagoras in particularly high esteem. He is of the
view that even though the Greeks stood at the very beginning then with respect to many scientific questions, still
their kind of research would be considered valid by a
strictly natural-scientific way of thinking. The Stoics and

Epicureans follow then in the second phase. They already represent a decline. They want ideas that stand in the service of life. In the New Academy, especially through the influence of Aenesidemus, Agrippa, and Sextus Empirikus one sees skepticism root out all belief in established scientific truths. And in Neo-Platonism, among philosophers like Ammonius Sakkas, Plotinus, Porphyrius, Jamblichus, and Proklus scientific research is replaced by a mystical experience straying into the labyrinthine passages of pseudophilosophy.

In the Middle Ages, though perhaps not so distinctly, one sees these four phases repeat themselves. With Thomas Aquinas a philosophically healthy way of picturing things begins, reviving Aristotelianism in a new form. In the next period, represented by Duns Scotus, an art of disputation holds sway—analogous to the first period of decline in Greek philosophy—that is taken to grotesque extremes. Then follows Nominalism, bearing a skeptical character. William of Occam rejects the view that universal ideas relate to anything real, and in doing so assigns to the content of human truth only the value of a conceptual summary standing outside of reality; whereas reality supposedly lies only in the particular individual things. This analogue of skepticism is replaced by the mysticism—no longer striving along scientific lines—of Eckhardt, Tauler, Heinrich Suso, the author of *German Theology*, and others. Those are the four phases of philosophical development in the Middle Ages.

In modern times, beginning with Bacon of Verulam, a healthy development begins again, based on natural-scientific thinking, in which then Descartes, Locke, and Leibnitz work further in a fruitful way. There follows the French and English philosophy of Enlightenment, in which principles, as one found them compatible with life, determined the style of the flow of philosophical thought. Then, with David Hume, skepticism appears; and following it, the phase of complete decay sets in, in England with Thomas Reid, in Germany with Kant. Brentano sees an aspect of Kant's philosophy that allows him to compare it with the Plotinian period of decadence in Greek philosophy. He criticizes Kant for not seeking truth in the agreement of our mental pictures with real objects as a scientific researcher does, but rather in believing that objects should conform to our human capacity for mental picturing. Brentano believes, therefore, that he must ascribe to Kant's philosophy a kind of basic mystical character that then manifests a totally unscientific nature in the decadent philosophy of Fichte, Schelling, and Hegel.

Brentano hopes for a new philosophical upsurge arising from a scientific work in the philosophical sphere modeled upon the natural-scientific way of thinking that has become dominant in modern times. As an introduction to such a philosophy, he set forth the thesis: True philosophical research cannot be of any other kind than that considered valid by the natural-scientific kind of cognition. He wanted to devote his life's work to this thesis.

In the preface to the reprint of the lecture in which he presented his view of the "four phases of philosophy," Brentano states that:

> His view of the history of philosophy might strike many people as ódd in its newness; for me, however, it has been an established fact for many years and has been the foundation of academic lectures in the history of philosophy given by me and several of my students now for more than two dec-

ades. I am under no illusion about the fact that my view will encounter prejudices and that these may perhaps be too strong to dispel with the first clash. Nevertheless, I hope that the facts and considerations I present cannot fail to make an impression upon anyone who pursues them thoughtfully.

It is altogether my opinion that one can receive a significant impression from Brentano's presentations. Insofar as from a particular point of view, they represent a classification of phenomena arising in the course of philosophical development, they are based on well-founded insights into the course taken by this development. The four phases of philosophy present differences that are founded within reality.

As soon as one enters into a study of the driving forces within the individual phases, however, one does not find that Brentano has accurately characterized these forces. This is evident at once in his insight about the first phase of the philosophy of antiquity. The basic features of Greek philosophy from its Ionic beginnings up to Aristotle do, indeed, reveal many features that justify Brentano in seeing in them what he considers to be a natural-scientific way of thinking. But does this way of thinking really arise from what Brentano calls the natural-scientific method? Are not the thoughts of this Greek philosophy far more a result of what they experienced in their own souls as the essential being of man and his relation to the world-all? Anyone who answers this question in accordance with the facts will find that the inner impulses for the thought content of this philosophy came to direct expression—precisely in Stoicism and Epicurianism—in the whole practical philosophy of life of later Greek times. One can see how, in the soul forces that

Brentano finds to be at work in the *second* phase, there lies the starting point for the first phase of the philosophy of antiquity. These forces were directed toward the sense-perceptible and social form of manifestations of the world-all, and therefore could only appear in an imperfect way in the phase of skepticism—which was driven to doubt the direct reality of this form of manifestation—and in the following phase of a seeing cognition, which must go beyond this form. For this reason these phases of ancient philosophy appear decadent.

And which soul forces are at work in the course of philosophical development in the Middle Ages? No one who really knows the relevant facts can doubt that Thomism represents the peak of this course of development with respect to those relationships that Brentano is investigating. But one cannot fail to recognize that, through the Christian standpoint of Thomas Aquinas, the soul forces at work in the Greek philosophy of life no longer operate merely out of philosophical impulses, but have taken on a more-than-philosophical character. What impulses are working in Thomas Aquinas insofar as he is a philosopher? One need have no sympathy for the weaknesses of the Nominalist philosophy of the Middle Ages; but one will indeed be able to discover that the soul impulses working in Nominalism also form the subjective basis for the Realism of Thomas. When Thomas recognizes the universal concepts synthesizing the phenomena of sense perception to be something that relates to a spiritually real element, he thus gains the strength for his Realistic way of picturing things out of his feeling for what these concepts signify within the existence of the soul itself, apart from the fact that they relate to sense phenomena. Precisely because Thomas did not relate the universal concepts directly to the events of sense-perceptible existence, he experienced how in these concepts another reality shines through to us, and how actually they are only signs for the phenomena of sense-perceptible life. Then, as this undertone of Thomism arose in Nominalism as an independent philosophy, this undertone naturally had to reveal its one-sidedness. The feeling that the concepts experienced in the soul establish a Realism in relation to the spirit had to disappear and the other feeling had to become dominant that the universal concepts are mere synthesizing names. When one sees the being of Nominalism in this way, one also understands the preceding second phase of medieval philosophy—that of Duns Scotus—as a transition to Nominalism. However, one cannot but understand the whole force of medieval thought work, *insofar as it is philosophy*, out of the basic view that revealed itself in a one-sided way in Nominalism. But then one will arrive at the view that the real driving forces of this philosophy lie in the soul impulses that, in keeping with Brentano's classification, one must designate as belonging to the *third* phase. And in that epoch which Brentano calls the mystical phase of the Middle Ages it becomes quite clear how the mystics belonging to it, persuaded of the Nominalistic nature of conceptual cognition, do not turn to this cognition but rather to other soul forces in order to penetrate to the core of the world's phenomena.

If, in line with Brentano's classification, we now pursue the activity of the driving soul forces in the philosophy of our time, we find that the inner character traits of this epoch are completely different from those indicated by Brentano. Because of certain of its own character traits, the phase of the natural-scientific way of thinking that Brentano finds realized in Bacon of Verulam, Descartes, Locke, and Leibnitz absolutely resists being thought of purely as natural-scientific in Brentano's sense. How can one deal in a purely natural-scientific way with Descartes' basic thought: "I think therefore I am;" how is one to bring Leibnitz's Monadology or his "predetermined harmony" into Brentano's way of picturing things? Even Brentano's view of the second phase, to which he assigns the French and English Enlightenment philosophy, creates difficulties when one wants to remain with his mental pictures. One would certainly not wish to deny to this epoch its character as a time of decadence in philosophy; but one can understand this epoch in light of the fact that, in its main representatives, those nonphilosophical soul impulses which were energetically at work in the Christian view of life were lamed, with the result that a relation to the supersensible world powers could not be found in a philosophical way. At the same time the Nominalistic skepticism of the Middle Ages worked on, preventing a search for a relation between the content of knowledge experienced in the soul and a spiritually real element.

And if we move on to modern skepticism and to that way of picturing things that Brentano assigns to the mystical stage, we then lose the possibility of still agreeing with his classification. To be sure, we must have the skeptical phase begin with David Hume. But the description of Kant, the "critical" thinker, as a mystic proves after all to be a too strongly one-sided characterization. Also, the philosophies of Fichte, Schelling, Hegel, and the other thinkers of the period after Kant cannot be regarded as mystical, especially if one bases oneself on Brentano's concept of mysticism. On the contrary, precisely in the sense of Brentano's classification, one will find a common basic impulse running from David Hume, through Kant, to Hegel. This impulse consists in the refusal, based on mental pictures gained in the sensory world, to depict any philosophical world picture of a true reality. As paradoxical as it may seem to call Hegel a skeptic, he is one after all in the sense that he ascribes no direct value as reality to the mental pictures taken from nature. One does not deviate from Brentano's concept of skepticism by regarding the development of philosophy from Hume to Hegel as the phase of modern skepticism. One can consider the fourth modern phase as beginning only after Hegel. Brentano, however, will certainly not wish to bring what arises there as the natural-scientific picture anywhere near mysticism. Still, look at the way Brentano himself wishes to situate himself with his philosophizing into this epoch. With an energy that could hardly be surpassed he demands a natural-scientific method in philosophy. In his psychological research he strives to keep to this method. And what he brings to light is a validation of anthroposophy. What would have to have arisen as the continuation of his anthropological striving, if he had gone further in the spirit of what he pictured, would be anthroposophy. An anthroposophy, to be sure, that stands in complete harmony with the natural-scientific way of thinking.

Is not Brentano's life work itself the most valid proof that the fourth phase of modern philosophy must draw its impulses from those soul forces that both Neo-Platonism and medieval mysticism *wished* to activate but *could* not, because they could not arrive with their inner soul activity at the kind of experience of spiritual reality that occurs with fully conscious clarity of thinking (or of concepts)? Just as Greek philosophy drew its strength from the soul impulses which Brentano sees as realizing themselves in the second philosophical phase out of a practical philosophy of living, and just as medieval philosophy owes its strength to the impulses of the third phase—that of skepticism—so must modern philosophy draw its impulses from the fundamental powers of the *fourth* phase—from that of a knowing seeing. If, in accordance with his way of picturing things, Brentano can regard Neo-Platonism and medieval mysticism as decadent philosophies, so one could recognize the anthroposophy that complements anthropology as the fruitful phase of modern philosophy, if one leads this philosopher's own ideas about the development of philosophy to their correct conclusions, which Brentano himself did not draw but which follow quite naturally from his ideas.

* * *

The picture we gave of Brentano's relation to the cognitional demands of our day explains why his reader receives impressions that are not limited to what is directly contained in the concepts he presents. Undertones sound forth all the time as one is reading. These emerge from a soul life that lies far deeper behind the ideas he expresses. What Brentano stimulates in the spirit of the reader often works more strongly in the latter than what the author expresses in sharply-edged pictures. One also feels moved to go back often and reread a book by Brentano. One may have thought through much of what is said today about the relation of philosophy to other cognitional views; Brentano's book *The Future of Philosophy*, will almost always rise up in one's memory when one is reflecting in this way. This is a reprint of a lecture to the Philosophical Society in Vienna in 1892 which he gave in order to oppose—with his view of the future of philosophy—what the jurist Adolf Exner had to say on this subject in his inaugural address on *Political Education* (1891). This publication of the lecture contains notes that offer far-ranging historical perspectives on the course of mankind's spiritual development. In this book all the tones are sounded of what can speak to an observer of today's natural-scientific outlook about the necessity of progressing from this outlook to an anthroposophical one.

The representatives of this natural-scientific way of picturing things live for the most part in the belief that this outlook is forced upon them by the real being of things. They are of the opinion that they organize their knowledge in accordance with the way reality manifests itself. In this belief they are deluding themselves, however. The truth is that in recent times the human soul—out of its own active development over thousands of years—has unfolded a need for the kind of mental pictures which comprise the natural-scientific picture of the world. It is not because reality presented this picture to them as the absolute truth that Helmholtz, Weisman, Huxley, and others arrived at their picture, but because they had to form this picture within themselves in order through it to shed a certain light upon the reality confronting them. It is not because of compulsion from a reality outside the soul that one forms a mathematical or mechanical picture of the world, but rather because one has given shape in one's soul to mathematical and mechanical pictures and thus opened an inner source of illumination for what manifests in the outer world in a mathematical and mechanical way.

Although generally what has just been described holds good for every developmental stage of the human soul, it does appear in the modern natural-scientific picture in a quite particular way. When these mental pictures are thought through consistently from a certain angle, they destroy any concepts of a soul element. This can be seen in the absolutely not trivial but most dubious concept of a "soul science without soul" that has not been thought up only by philosophical dilettantes but also by very serious thinkers.* The mental pictures formed by natural science are leading to ever more insight into the dependency of the phenomena of ordinary consciousness upon our bodily organization. If the fact is not recognized at the same time that what arises in this way as the soul element is *not* this soul element itself, but only its manifestation in a mirror image, then the true idea of the soul element slips away from our observation, and the illusory idea arises that sees in the soul element only a product of the bodily organization. On the other hand, however, this latter view cannot stand up before an unbiased thinking. To this unbiased thinking, the ideas that natural science forms about nature show a soul connection—to a reality lying behind nature—that does *not* reveal itself in these ideas themselves. No anthropological approach, out of itself, can arrive at thorough-going mental pictures of this soul connection. For, it does not enter ordinary consciousness.

This fact shows up much more strongly in today's natural-scientific outlook than was the case in earlier historical stages of knowledge. At these earlier stages, when observing the outer world, one still formed concepts that took up

* This picture of a "soul science without soul" also belongs to the realm of the riddles described in this book as existing at the "borderland of our knowing activity"; and if this picture is not experienced in such a way that it is taken as the starting point of a seeing consciousness, it then walls off the entryway to true knowing of the soul, instead of showing a path to such knowing.

into their content something of the spiritual foundations of this outer world. And one's soul felt itself, in its own spirituality, as unified with the spirit of the outer world. In accordance with its own essential being, recent natural scientists must think nature in a purely natural way. Through this, to be sure, it gains the possibility of validating the *content* of its ideas by observation of nature, but not the *existence* of these ideas themselves, as something with inner soul being.

For this reason, precisely the genuine natural-scientific outlook has no foundation if it cannot validate its own existence by anthroposophical observation. *With* anthroposophy one can fully endorse the natural-scientific outlook; *without* anthroposophy, one will again and again want to make the vain attempt to discover even the spirit out of the results of natural-scientific observation. The natural-scientific ideas of recent times are in fact the results of the soul's living together with a spiritual world; but only in living spiritual vision can the soul *know* about its living together with that world.*

The question could easily arise: Then why does the soul seek to form natural-scientific pictures, if precisely through them it is creating for itself a content that cuts it off from its spiritual foundation? From the standpoint of the beliefs that see the natural-scientific outlook to have been formed in accordance with the way the world does in fact manifest to us, there is no way to find an answer to this question. But an

---

* Where the genuine natural-scientific approach leads is convincingly shown in a book by Oskar Hertwig, which is outstanding in many respects, *The Development of Organisms, a Refutation of Darwin's Theory of Chance*, 1916. Precisely when a work, like that underlying this book, is so exemplary in its application of the natural-scientific method, it can lead to innumerable soul experiences at the "boundaries of our knowing activity."

answer is definitely forthcoming if one looks toward the needs of the soul itself. With mental pictures, such as only could have been formed by a pre-natural-scientific age, our soul experience could never have arrived at a full consciousness of itself. In its ideas of nature, which also continued a spiritual element, it would indeed have felt an indefinite connection with the spirit, but it would not have been able to experience the spirit in its own full, independent, and particular nature. Therefore, in the course of mankind's development, our soul element strives to set forth the kind of ideas that do not contain this soul element itself, in order, through them, to know *itself* as independent of natural existence. The connection with the spirit, however, must then be sought in knowledge not through these ideas of nature but through spiritual vision. The development of modern natural science is a necessary stage in the course of mankind's soul evolution. One understands the basis of this development when one sees how the soul needs it in order to find itself. On the other hand, one recognizes the epistemological implications of this development when one sees how precisely *it* makes spiritual vision a necessity.*

Adolf Exner, whose views are opposed by Brentano's book *The Future of Philosophy*, confronted a natural science that wishes, it is true, to develop its ideas of nature in purity, but that is not prepared to advance to anthroposophy when it is a matter of grasping the reality of the soul. Exner found "natural-scientific education" to be unfruitful in developing

---

* What is expressed here is presented in a detailed way in my book *The Riddles of Philosophy*. One of the basic thoughts of that book is to show how natural-scientific cognition proves its power in the soul progress of humanity.

104

ideas that must work in the way people live together in human society. For solving the questions of social life facing us in the future, therefore, he demands a way of thinking that does not rest on a natural-scientific basis. He finds that the great juridical questions confronting the Romans were solved by them in such a fruitful way because they had little gift for the natural-scientific way of picturing things. And he attempts to show that the eighteenth century, in spite of its attraction to the natural-scientific way of thinking, proved quite inadequate in mastering social questions. Exner directs his gaze upon a natural-scientific outlook that is not striving scientifically to understand its own foundation. It is understandable that he arrived at the views he did when confronted by such an outlook. For, this outlook must develop its ideas in such a way that they bring before the soul what is of nature in all its purity. From such ideas no impulse is gained for thoughts that are fruitful in social life. For, in social life souls confront each other as souls. Such an impulse can arise only when the soul element, in its spiritual nature, is experienced through a knowing vision (*erkennendes Schauen*), when the natural-scientific, anthropological view finds its complement in anthro-posophy.

Brentano bore ideas in his soul that definitely lead into the anthroposophical realm in spite of the fact that he wished to remain only in the anthropological realm. This is why the arguments he mounts against Exner are so pene-trating, even though Brentano does not wish to make the transition to anthroposophy himself. They show how Exner does not speak at all about the real abilities of a natural-sci-entific outlook that understands itself; they show how he tilted with windmills in his battle against a way of thinking

105

that misunderstands itself. One can read Brentano's book and everywhere feel in it how justified everything is that points through his ideas in one direction or another, without finding that he expresses fully what it is that he is pointing toward.

With Franz Brentano a personality has left us whose work, when experienced, can mean an immeasurable gain. This gain is completely independent of the degree of intellectual agreement that one brings to this work. For, this gain springs from the manifestations of a human soul that have their source much deeper in the world's reality than that sphere in which in ordinary life, intellectual agreement is to be found. And Brentano is a personality destined to work on in the course of humanity's spiritual development through impulses that are not limited to the extension of the ideas he developed. I can very well imagine someone's total disagreement with what I have presented here as Brentano's relation to anthroposophy; regardless of one's scientific standpoint, however, it seems to me impossible—if one lets work upon oneself the philosophical spirit that breathes through the writings of this man—that one could arrive at anything less than the feelings of high esteem for the value of Brentano's personality that underly the intentions of this essay.

Sketches of Some of the Ramifications of the Content of this Book

Addendum 1 to pages 13 and 24:
The Philosophical Validation of Anthroposophy

Anyone who wishes his cognitive approach to be grounded in the philosophical thinking of the present day must justify epistemologically—to himself and to that thinking—the actual soul element referred to in the first chapter of this book. Of the people who recognize the real soul element from direct inner experience and who know how to distinguish it from soul experiences caused by the senses, few are asking for any such justification. Such justification often seems to them to be an unnecessary or even bothersome conceptual hairsplitting. Contrasting with their kind of aversion is the antipathy of philosophical thinkers. They want to regard our inner experience of the soul element as merely subjective, with no claim to scientific value. They therefore have little inclination, in the realm of their philosophical concepts, to seek the elements by which to approach anthroposophical ideas. This aversion, coming from both sides, makes understanding extraordinarily difficult. For, in our time, a scientific value can be ascribed to a cognitive approach only if this approach can validate its views before the same tribunal at which natural-scientific laws seek their justification.

For an epistemological justification of anthroposophical ideas, the essential point is to express in the most *exact possible concepts* the way these ideas are experienced. We can do this in the most varied ways. Let us attempt to describe two of these ways here. As to the first way, let us start with

107

a consideration of memory. In doing so, we encounter at once a problematical point in modern philosophical knowledge. For, very few clear concepts about the nature of memory are operative there. I will take my start from ideas which, it is true, I have discovered on anthroposophical paths, but which can be thoroughly substantiated by philosophy and physiology. The space I can allow myself in this book, to be sure, is not sufficient for such a substantiation. I hope to present one in a future book. I believe, however, that anyone able to grasp the current findings of physiology and psychology correctly will find what I am going to say about memory to be well-founded.

The mental pictures stimulated by sense impressions enter the realm of unconscious human experience. From there, these pictures can be brought back up; they can be remembered. Mental pictures are of a purely soul nature; but consciousness of them in ordinary waking life is dependent upon the body. Furthermore, the soul bound to the body cannot, through the soul's own forces, lift these pictures out of their unconscious state into a conscious one. For this the soul needs the forces of the body. In ordinary memory the body must be active, just as it must be active in order for sensory pictures to arise in the processes of the sense organs. For me to see a sense-perceptible occurrence, a bodily activity must first develop within the sense organs; produced by them, a picture arises in the soul. For me to remember such a picture, an inner bodily activity (in delicate organs), which is the polar opposite of sense activity, must occur, and as a consequence, the remembered picture arises in the soul. This picture is connected to a sense-perceptible occurrence that stood before my soul in the past. I picture this occurrence through an inner experience that my bodily organization makes possible. Now focus on the nature of such a memory picture. For, through this one can grasp the nature of anthroposophical ideas. These ideas are not memory pictures; but they appear in the soul in the same way as memory pictures do. This is a disappointment for many people who would like to acquire pictures of the spiritual world in a more robust form. But one cannot experience the spiritual world in a form more substantial than that in which, in memory, one experiences a past sense-perceptible event that is no longer visible to one. Now this ability to remember such an event stems from the power of our bodily organization. This organization must play no part, however, in our experience of the actual soul element. Rather, the soul must awaken within itself the ability to accomplish with mental pictures what the body accomplishes with sensory pictures when it conveys the recollection of these sensory pictures. Such mental pictures—which are brought up from the depths of the soul entirely by the power of the soul just as memory pictures are raised from the depths of human nature by our bodily organization— are mental pictures that relate to the spiritual world. They are present in every soul. What must be acquired in order for us to become aware of their presence is the power, purely through the activation of our soul, to bring these mental pictures up from the depths of the soul. As remembered sensory pictures relate to a past sense impression, so these mental pictures relate to a connection—not present in the sense world—of the soul with the spiritual world. The human soul stands in the same relation to the spiritual world as a person ordinarily does to a forgotten reality; and the soul comes to know this world when it awakens powers

109

within itself that are similar to the bodily powers which serve memory.

The essential point, therefore, in the philosophical justification of ideas about the true soul element, is to investigate our inner life in such a way that we find within it an activity which is purely of a soul nature but yet in a certain respect is similar to the activity unfolded in remembering.

A second way to form a concept of a purely soul element is this. One can focus upon the findings of anthropology when it observes a person exercising will (acting). To begin with, the mental picture of the deed underlies the intended will impulse. This mental picture is known physiologically to be dependent upon the bodily organization (the nervous system). A nuance of feeling, a feeling of sympathy with what is pictured, is connected with the mental picture, and causes the mental picture to provide the impulse for action. But then the soul experience loses itself in the depths and only the result arises again consciously. The human being sees how he moves his body in order to perform what he has pictured. (Th. Ziehen has presented all this with particular clarity in his physiological psychology.)

One can see from this how, when an act of will comes into question, our conscious life in mental pictures ceases with respect to the intermediary element of *will*. What is experienced in the soul as we will an action performed by the body does not enter our ordinary conscious life of mental pictures. But it is also obvious that such a will impulse realizes itself through the activity of the body. It is also not difficult to recognize that the soul unfolds a will activity when, following logical laws, it seeks truth by connecting mental pictures to each other; a will activity that physiological laws cannot encompass. Otherwise, an illogical connection of mental pictures—or even a merely a-logical one—could not be distinguished from one that takes a logically lawful course. (Dilettantish claims that logical deduction is merely a characteristic acquired by the soul through adaptation to the outer world is not worthy of serious consideration.) In this will activity, which runs its course purely within the soul, and which leads to logically grounded convictions, we can see a permeation of the soul with a purely spiritual activity. Our ordinary mental picturing knows as little what occurs in our outward directed will as a sleeping person knows about himself. But we are also not as fully conscious of the logical determining factors by which we form our convictions as we are of the actual content of our convictions. Anyone who knows, even anthropologically, how to observe inwardly is able, after all, in ordinary consciousness, to recognize the presence of logical determinants. He will realize that the human being knows this logical determination the way he knows something *in dreams*. One is totally justified in declaring the correctness of the paradox: ordinary consciousness knows the content of its convictions; but it only dreams the logical lawfulness that lives in the seeking of these convictions. We can see: in ordinary consciousness we *sleep through* the will element when unfolding will to act outwardly through the body; we *dream through* our will activity when seeking convictions through thinking. And we know, in fact, that in this latter case what we are dreaming cannot be of a bodily nature, for then logical laws would have to coincide with physiological laws. If we form the concept of a will activity living in a thinking quest for truth, then we are conceiving of something with real soul being.

From these two epistemological approaches to the concept of real soul being in an anthroposophical sense (other approaches are also possible), we can see how far removed this essential soul being is from anything in the nature of abnormal soul activity such as visionary, hallucinatory, or mediumistic states. For, the source of all such abnormalities must be sought in the physiological realm. The soul element described by anthroposophy, however, is not only of the same kind as our soul experiences in normal healthy consciousness; within the full waking consciousness of mental picturing, we can also experience this soul element in a way similar to that of remembering past events in our life, or of arriving at convictions that are logically determined. From this we can see clearly that anthroposophy's cognitive experience runs its course in mental pictures that retain the character of ordinary consciousness which is endowed with reality from the outer world; and to this ordinary consciousness anthroposophy adds abilities that lead into the spiritual realm; everything of a visionary, hallucinatory nature, on the other hand, lives in a consciousness that adds nothing to our ordinary one but that takes abilities away from this ordinary consciousness, causing our state of consciousness to sink below the level present in conscious sense perception. For those readers who know what I have written in other books about memory and recollection, I would like to add the following. The mental pictures that have entered our unconscious and can be recollected later are to be found—as mental pictures during the time they are unconscious—within that part of the human being which in those books is called the life body (etheric body). The activity, however, through which the mental pictures anchored in the life body are recollected belongs to the physical body. I add this comment so that those who are quick to jump to conclusions will not construe as a contradiction what is in fact a distinction demanded by the nature of the case.

Addendum 2 to page 16:
The Appearance of Limits to Knowledge

Thinkers who strive with all their strength to gain the kind of relation to true reality that is demanded by the inner nature of the human being discuss a great number of the limits to knowledge referred to on page 16ff.; and if one looks at the nature of these discussions, one can see quite clearly that the thrust experienced by genuine thinkers in their encounter with such "limits" is in the direction of that inner soul experience which is the subject of this first essay. Take a look, for example, at the way the gifted thinker Friedrich Theodore Vischer, in the important essay he wrote on Johannes Volkelt's book *Dream Fantasy*, describes the cognitive experience he had in the encounter with one such limit:

"No spirit where there is no nerve center, where there is no brain," declare our opponents. "No nerve center, no brain," we reply, "if not evolved from below upward, through innumerable levels." It is easy to speak scornfully of mind (spirit) hovering about in granite and limestone, no more difficult than it would be for us to ask scornfully how protein in the brain can wing its way up to ideas. Measuring the different levels defies human knowledge. It will forever remain a secret how it happens that nature—beneath whose surface, after all, the spirit must be slumbering—stands there as so complete a counterstroke of the spirit that we bruise ourselves against it; this separation seems so absolute that Hegel's formulation, as brilliant as it is, of something "other than," or "outside of," oneself is as good as meaningless and only hides the extreme nature of this wall of seeming separation. One does find in Fichte's work a true recognition of the cutting edge and blows of this counterstroke, but no explanation for it.

(See Friedrich Theodore Vischer, *Views Old and New*, 1881.) Friedrich Theodore Vischer points vigorously to one of the places to which anthroposophy must also point. But the fact does not enter his consciousness that at such a borderland of knowledge a different form of knowing activity can enter. He wishes to live at these borderlands in the same kind of knowing activity which sufficed for him before he arrived at them. Anthroposophy attempts to show that science does not end where our ordinary knowing activity gets "bruised," where these "cuts and blows" occur in the counterstroke of reality; anthroposophy tries to show that the experiences resulting from these "bruises, cuts, and blows" lead to the development of a different kind of knowing activity, which transforms the counterthrust of reality into a spiritual perception that, to begin with, on its first level, is comparable to tactile perception in the sense world.

In the third section of *Views Old and New*, Friedrich Theodore Vischer states: "Good, there is no soul alongside of the body (Vischer means for the materialist); thus, precisely what we make a point of calling 'matter'—at the highest level of its formation known to us: in the brain—becomes soul, and the soul evolves into spirit. We are supposed to form a concept [of matter], which to the analyzing intellect is in complete contradiction with itself." Again anthroposophy must reply to Vischer's presentation: Good, for the intellect that breaks things down into their component parts, there is a contradiction here; but for the *soul*, this

115

contradiction becomes the point of departure for an activity of knowing at which the analyzing intellect halts because this intellect experiences the "counterstroke" of spiritual reality.

Gideon Spicker, who, besides a number of other astute books, has also written *Philosophical Confessions of a Former Capuchin Monk* (1910), points to one of the borderlands of our ordinary knowing activity (using words that are certainly vivid enough):

> No matter what one's philosophy is, whether dogmatic or skeptical, empirical or transcendental, critical or eclectic, they all, without exception, take their start from an unproven and unprovable premise: the *essentiality of thinking.* No investigation will ever get behind this essentiality, no matter how deep it may dig. This essentiality must be accepted unconditionally and cannot be substantiated by anything; any attempt to prove its validity only presupposes this essentiality. Under it there gapes a bottomless abyss, a frightful darkness unlit by any ray of light. We do not know, therefore, where it comes from or where it is leading. Whether a merciful God or an evil demon has laid this essentiality into our reason is equally uncertain.

Thus, even the contemplation of thinking itself leads the thinker to the limits of ordinary knowledge. Anthroposophy sets in with its knowing activity at these limits; it knows that essentiality confronts the abilities (art) of intellectual thinking like an impenetrable wall. For a thinking *that the thinker experiences,* however, the impenetrability of this wall disappears; this experienced thinking finds a light with which to illuminate *and look into* the "darkness unlit by any ray of light" of a merely intellectual thinking; and the "bottomless abyss" is so only for the realm of sense perception; anyone who does not halt at this abyss but dares to proceed with thinking even when this thinking must set aside what the sense world has inserted into it, such a person finds a spiritual reality in this "bottomless abyss."

We could continue indefinitely like this, presenting the experiences that serious thinkers have at the limits of knowledge.

Such examples would show that anthroposophy is the natural result of the evolution of present-day thought. Many things point to anthroposophy if these many things are seen in the right light.

Addendum 3 to page 19:
The Abstractness of Our Concepts

In this essay, I speak about the "laming" of our mental pictures when they merely copy sense-perceptible reality.

The real facts behind the working of abstraction in our cognitive process are to be sought in this laming. The human being forms concepts about sense-perceptible reality. For epistemology [the science that investigates our knowing activity] the question arises: How does what man retains in his soul as a concept of a real being or process relate to this real being or process? Is what I carry around in me as concept of a wolf equivalent to any reality, or is it merely a schema, formed by my soul, which I have made for myself by noting (abstracting) the characteristics of one or another wolf, but which does not correspond to anything in the real world? This question received extensive consideration in the medieval dispute between the Nominalists and the Realists. For the Nominalists, the only thing real about a wolf is the visible substance, flesh, blood, bones, etc., present in this one particular wolf. The concept "wolf" is "merely" a mental summation of characteristics common to the various wolves. The *Realist* replies to this: Any substance you find in a particular wolf is also present in other animals. There must be something else in addition that orders substance into the living coherency found in a wolf. This ordering real element is given through the concept.

One must admit that Vincenz Knauer, the outstanding expert on Aristotle and medieval philosophy, said something exceptional in his book *The Main Problems of Philosophy* (Vienna, 1892) when discussing Aristotelian epistemology:

A wolf, for example, does not consist of any material components different from those of a lamb; its
material corporeality is built up out of the lamb
flesh it has assimilated; but the wolf does not become a lamb, even if it eats nothing but lamb its
whole life long. *What makes it into a wolf, therefore,
must obviously be something other than hyle, sense-perceptible matter; and indeed it must not and cannot be any
mere thing of thought, although it is accessible only to
thinking and not to the senses; it must be something
working [productive] and therefore actual—something
very real.*

But how, in the sense of a merely anthropological investigation, could one wish to attain the reality indicated here?
What is communicated to the soul by the senses does not
produce the concept "wolf." But what is present in ordinary
consciousness as this concept is definitely not something
"working" [productive]. Through the power of this concept,
the assembling of the sense-perceptible materials united in
a wolf could certainly not occur. The truth is that this question takes anthropology beyond the limits of its ability to
know. Anthroposophy shows that along with the relation of
man to wolf in the sense-perceptible realm, there exists
another one as well. This other relation, in its own particular, direct nature, does not enter our ordinary consciousness. But this relation does exist as a *living* supersensible
connection between man and the object he perceives with
his senses. The living element that exists in man through
this connection is lamed, reduced to a "concept" by his
intellectual organization. The abstract mental picture is this
real element—which has died in order to present itself to
ordinary consciousness—in which man does live during

119

sense perception, but whose living quality does not become conscious. The abstractness of our mental pictures is caused by an inner necessity of the soul. Reality gives man something living. He deadens that part of this living element which enters his ordinary consciousness. He does so because he could not achieve self-consciousness in his encounter with the outer world if he had to experience his actual connection to this outer world in its full vitality. Without the laming of this full vitality, man would have to recognize himself as one part within a unity extending beyond his human limits; he would be an organ of a greater organism.

The way man lets his cognitive process turn, inwardly, into the abstractness of concepts is *not* caused by something real lying outside of him, but rather by the developmental requirements of his own being, which demand that, in his process of perception, he dampen down his living connection with the outer world into these abstract concepts that provide the foundation upon which self-consciousness arises. The fact that this is so reveals itself to the soul after the development of its spiritual organs. Through this development, the living connection with a spiritual reality lying outside man is reestablished; but if self-consciousness were not already something acquired by ordinary consciousness, self-consciousness could not be developed within a seeing consciousness.[*] One can understand from this that a healthy ordinary consciousness is the necessary prerequisite for a seeing consciousness. Someone who believes himself able to develop a seeing consciousness without an active and healthy ordinary consciousness is very much in error. In

---

[*] *Das schauende Bewusstsein*: i.e., a consciousness that not only thinks the spirit but sees it with spiritual organs as well. Translator.

fact, ordinary normal consciousness must accompany seeing consciousness at every moment; otherwise the latter would bring disorder into human self-consciousness and therefore into man's relation to reality. Anthroposophy, with its seeing knowledge, can have to do only with this kind of consciousness, but not with any dimming down of ordinary consciousness.

[Editor's addendum: On January 27, 1923, in Dornach, Rudolf Steiner had the following to say about "concepts" and the Scholastic "Realists":

The Realists said: The ideas, concepts, and forms in which sense-perceptible matter is ordered are realities. To be sure, for the Schoolmen, these ideas and concepts had already become abstractions. But they considered these abstractions to be something real because their abstractions were descendants of earlier, much more concrete and substantial views. In an earlier age, human beings did not look merely upon the concept "wolf." They looked upon the real group soul "wolf" present in the spiritual world. This was a real being. For the Schoolmen, this real being had grown insubstantial and become an abstract concept. But in spite of this, the Realistic Schoolmen still had the feeling that the concept was not empty of content, but rather contained something real.

This real element, to be sure, was descended from earlier beings who were totally real. But one still sensed the kinship, in exactly the same way that Plato experienced his ideas—which also were much more alive and substantial than the medieval Scholastic ideas—as descended from the old Persian

121

archangelic beings who, as Amshaspands, lived and worked in the universe. Those were very real beings. For Plato, they were already hazy, and for the medieval Schoolmen they were abstractions. That was the last stage at which the ancient clairvoyance had arrived. Certainly, medieval Realistic Scholasticism was no longer based on clairvoyance; but what it had preserved in its traditions as real concepts and ideas—living everywhere in stones, plants, animals, and physical human beings—was still regarded, in fact, as something spiritual, no matter how diluted that spiritual element had become. The Nominalists—because in fact the age of abstraction, of intellectualism, was approaching—had already become aware that they were no longer able to connect something real to ideas or concepts. For them, concepts and ideas were mere names to make categorization easier.]

Addendum 4 to Page 22:
An Important Characteristic of Spiritual Perception

The soul's perceptions in the realm of spiritual reality do not live on in the soul in the same way as those mental pictures do that are gained from sense perceptions. Although a comparison of spiritual perceptions with memory pictures is possible—as was shown in the first addendum to this essay—spiritual perceptions do not act like memory pictures in the soul. What is experienced as a spiritual perception *cannot*, in fact, be retained in this direct form as a memory picture can. If a person is to have the same spiritual perception anew, the perception must also be *produced* anew in the soul. This means that the relation of the soul to the pertinent spiritual reality must be sought again. And this renewal cannot be compared with the memory of a sense impression; it can only be compared to confronting the eye again with the same sense-perceptible object that made an earlier impression. What can be retained directly in one's memory from a real spiritual perception is not this memory itself, but rather the soul activity by which one attained the perception in question. If I am striving to renew a spiritual perception from the past, I do not seek a memory of this perception; I seek the memory that recalls the soul activity that led to the perception in the first place. The perception occurs then through a process that is independent of me. It is important to be fully conscious of these two different processes, because only through this consciousness can one achieve a correct knowledge of what is really *spiritually objective*.

The nature of these two processes is modified in actual practice, however, through the fact that the content of spiritual perception can be transferred from seeing consciousness into ordinary consciousness. This content then turns into an abstract mental picture in ordinary consciousness. And *this mental picture* can be remembered in the usual way.

But, precisely by careful training in the recognition of the following distinctions, which arise in the soul's life with a certain subtlety, one can achieve much in the way of a rightful, conscious relation of the soul to the spiritual world:

1. soul processes that lead to a spiritual perception
2. spiritual perceptions themselves
3. spiritual perceptions that are transformed into the concepts present in ordinary consciousness.

Addendum 5 to page 71:
The Real Basis of an Intentional Relation

With the "intentional relation" characterized in chapter 3, a soul element enters into Brentano's psychology but *only as a fact* of ordinary consciousness, without this fact being further explained and incorporated into our experience of the soul. I would like to be allowed here to sketch out some things about this fact that are based for me upon views that I have worked out in many different directions. To be sure, these views still need to be brought into more detailed form and to be fully substantiated. My situation until now, however, has only made it possible for me to present certain salient points in lectures. What I can bring here are only some *findings* sketched out in brief. And I beg the reader to take them *as such* for now. These are not "sudden fancies"; We are dealing here with something that I have worked for years to substantiate, employing the scientific means of our day.

In that soul experience which Franz Brentano calls "judging," an acceptance or rejection of our mental pictures comes to meet this mere mental picturing (that consists in an inner shaping of pictures). The question arises for the soul researcher: What is it in our soul experience by which there does not merely arise the mental picture "green tree," but also the judgment "this is a green tree"? The *something* that accomplishes this cannot lie within the narrower circle of our life in mental pictures circumscribed by our ordinary consciousness. The fact that we cannot find it here has led to the epistemological thought that I describe in the second volume of my *Riddles of Philosophy* in the chapter "The World as Illusion." At issue here is an experience lying outside this circle. The point is to discover the "where" in the realm of our soul experiences.

When a person is confronting a sense-perceptible object and unfolding his activity of perception, this *something* cannot be found anywhere in all that he receives in the process of perception in such a way that this receiving is grasped through the physiological and psychological pictures that relate to the outer object on the one hand, and to the pertinent sense organ on the other. When someone has the visual perception "green tree," the fact of the judgment "this is a green tree" cannot be found in any directly evident physiological or psychological relation between "tree" and "eye." What is experienced in the soul as the inner fact of *judging* is actually an additional relation between the "person" and the "tree" different from the relation between "tree" and "eye." Nevertheless, only the latter relation is experienced in all its sharpness in ordinary consciousness. The other relation remains in a dim state of subconsciousness and only comes to light in its result as the *recognition* of the "green tree" as something that exists. With every perception that comes to a head as a judgment one is dealing with a *twofold relation* of man to objectivity.

One gains insight into this twofold relation only if one can replace today's fragmentary science of the senses with a complete one. Anyone who takes into consideration everything that pertains to a characterization of a human sense organ will find that one must call other things "senses" besides what is usually designated as such. What makes the "eye" a "sense organ," for example, is also present when one experiences the fact that someone else's 'I' is observed or that someone else's thought is recognized as such. With respect to such facts one usually errs in not making a thor-

126

oughly justified and necessary distinction. One believes, for example, that when hearing the words of another person, it suffices to speak of a "sense" only insofar as "hearing" comes into question and that everything else is to be ascribed to a nonsensory, inner activity. But that is not the actual state of affairs. In hearing human words and understanding them as thoughts, a threefold activity comes into consideration. And each component of this threefold activity must be studied in its own right, if a valid scientific view is to arise. Hearing is one of these activities. But hearing as such is just as little a perception of words as touching is a seeing. And if, in accordance with the facts, one distinguishes between the sense of touch and the sense of sight, one must also make distinctions between hearing, perceiving words, and then apprehending the thought. It leads to a faulty psychology and to a faulty epistemology if one does not make a sharp distinction between our apprehension of a thought and our thought activity, and if one does not recognize the sensory nature of the former. One makes this mistake only because the organ by which we perceive a word and that by which we apprehend a thought are not as outwardly perceptible as the ear is for hearing. In reality sense organs are present for these two activities of perception just as the ear is present for hearing. If one follows through on what physiology and psychology can find in this regard if they investigate fully, one arrives at the following view of the human sense organization. One must distinguish: the sense for the 'I' of another person; the sense for apprehending thoughts; the sense for perceiving words; the sense of hearing; the sense of warmth; the sense of sight; the sense of taste; the sense of smell; the sense of balance (the perceptive experience of finding oneself in a certain state of equilib-

127

rium with respect to the outer world); the sense of movement (the perceptive experience of the resting state or
movement of one's own limbs on the one hand, and the
state of rest or movement with respect to the outer world;
the sense of life (the experience of the state of one's own
organism; the feeling of how one is); the sense of touch. All
these senses bear the traits which lead us, in truth, to call
eyes and ears "senses."

Anyone who does not acknowledge the validity of these
distinctions falls into disorder in his knowledge of reality.
With his mental pictures, he succumbs to the fate of their
not allowing him to experience anything truly real. For
someone, for example, who calls the *eye a sense* but assumes
no sense organ for the perception of words, even the picture
he forms of the eye will remain an unreal configuration.

I believe that Fritz Mauthner, in his critique of language,
speaks in his clever way of a "sense for chance" only because he is looking at a fragmentary science of the human
senses. If this were not the case, he would notice how a
sense organ places itself into reality.

Now, when a person confronts a sense-perceptible object, the situation is such that he never receives an impression through only one sense, but always through *at least one
other* sense as well from the series listed above. The relation
to *one* sense enters ordinary consciousness with particular
distinctness; the relation to the other sense remains *dimmer*.
A distinction exists between the senses, however: a number
of the senses allow our relation to the outer world to be
experienced more as an outer one; the other senses allow us
to experience the outer world more as something closely
connected to our own existence. The senses that find themselves in close connection to our own existence are, for

128

example, our sense of balance, our sense of movement, our sense of life, and even our sense of touch. In the perceptions of these senses with respect to the outer world, our own existence is dimly felt along with them. Yes, one could say that a dullness of our conscious perceiving occurs just because the relation out into the world is drowned out by the experiencing of our own being. If there occurs the *seeing* of an object, for example, and at the same time our sense of balance is communicating an impression, what is seen will be sharply perceived. What is seen leads to a mental picture of the object. As a perception, our experience through the sense of balance remains dull; nevertheless it manifests in the judgment that "what I see exists" or "that is what I see."

In reality, things do not stand beside each other in abstract differentiation; they pass over into one another with their characteristics. Thus it comes about that, in the full complement of our senses, there are some that transmit less a relation to the outer world and more an experience of one's own being. These latter senses dip down more into our inner soul life than do, say, the eye or ear; therefore the results of what they transmit as perceptions appear as inner soul experiences. However, even with them, one should distinguish the actual soul element from the perceptual element just as, when seeing something, for example, one distinguishes the outer fact from the inner soul experiences one has in connection with it.

Anyone who takes the anthroposophical point of view must not shrink from such subtle distinctions in mental pictures like those made here. He must be able to distinguish between perceiving the word and hearing, on the one hand, and between perceiving the word and understanding it through his own thoughts, on the other, just as ordinary consciousness distinguishes between a tree and a rock. If one would take this more into account, one would recognize that anthroposophy does not just have the one aspect—usually called the mystical side—but also the other, by which anthroposophy leads to a research no less scientific than that of natural science; it leads in fact to a more scientific approach which requires a more subtle and more methodological elaboration of our life in mental pictures than even ordinary philosophy does. I believe that in his philosophical research Wilhelm Dilthey was on his way to the science of the senses that I have sketched out here, but that he could not attain his goal because he did not push through to a complete elaboration of the pertinent mental pictures. (Please see what I said about this in my *Riddles of Philosophy*).

Addendum 6 to page 74:
The Physical and Spiritual Dependencies of Man's Being

I would also like now to sketch out what I have discovered about the relations of the soul element to the physical-bodily element. I can indeed state that I am describing here the results of a thirty-year-long spiritual-scientific investigation. Only in recent years has it become possible for me to grasp the pertinent elements in thoughts expressible in words in such a way that I could bring what I was striving for to a provisional conclusion. I would also like to allow myself to present the results of my investigation in the form of indications only. It is fully possible to substantiate these results with the scientific means available today. This would be the subject of a lengthy book, which circumstances do not allow me to write at this time.

If one is seeking the relation of the soul element to the bodily element, one cannot base oneself upon Brentano's division of our soul experiences—described on page 69ff. of this book—into mental picturing, judging, and the phenomena of loving and hating. In the search for the pertinent relations, this division leads to such a skewing of the relevant circumstances that one cannot obtain results that accord with the facts. In an investigation like ours, one must take one's start from the division rejected by Brentano: into mental picturing,[*] feeling, and willing. If one now draws together all of the soul element that is experienced as mental picturing, and seeks the bodily processes with which this soul element is related, one finds the appropriate connec-

---

[*] *Vorstellen* here is virtually synonymous with "thinking." Ed.

tion by being able to link up, to a considerable extent, with the results of today's physiological psychology. The bodily counterparts of the soul element of mental picturing are to be found in the processes of the nervous system, with its extensions into the sense organs on the one hand and into the internal organization of the body on the other. No matter how much, from the anthroposophical viewpoint, one will have to think many things differently than modern science does, this science does provide an excellent foundation.

This is not the case when one wishes to determine the bodily counterparts of feeling and willing. With respect to them one must first pave the right path within the realm of the findings of today's physiology. If one has achieved the right path, one finds that just as one must relate mental picturing to nerve activity, so one must also relate feeling to that life rhythm which is centered in the breathing activity and is connected with it. In doing so one must bear in mind that, for our purposes, one must follow the breathing rhythm, with all that is connected with it, right into the most peripheral parts of our organization. In order to achieve concrete results in this region, the results of physiological research must be pursued in a direction that is still quite unusual today. Only when one accomplishes this will all those contradictions disappear which result at first when feeling and the breathing rhythm are brought together. What at first inspires contradiction turns out, upon deeper study, to be a proof of this relation.

Let us just take one example from the extensive region that must be explored here. The experience of music is based on feeling. The content of musical configurations, however, lives in our mental picturing,[*] which is transmitted through the perceptions of hearing. Through what does the musical feeling experience arise? The *mental picture* of the tone configuration, which is based on the organ of hearing and on a nerve process, is not yet this musical experience. This latter arises through the fact that in the brain the breathing rhythm—in its extension up into this organ—encounters what is accomplished by the ear and nervous system. And the soul lives then not merely in what is heard and pictured; it lives in the breathing rhythm; it experiences what is released in the breathing rhythm through the fact that what is occurring in the nervous system strikes upon this rhythmical life, so to speak. One need only see the physiology of the breathing rhythm in the right light and one will arrive at a comprehensive recognition of the statement: The soul has feeling experiences by basing itself upon the breathing rhythm in the same way it bases itself, in mental picturing, upon nerve processes.

And relative to willing one finds that it is based, in a similar way, upon metabolic processes. Here again, one must include in one's study all the pertinent ramifications and extensions of the metabolic processes within the entire organism. Just as, when something is *mentally pictured*, a nerve process occurs upon which the soul becomes conscious of its mental picturing, and just as, when something is *felt*, a modification of the breathing rhythm takes place through which a feeling arises in the soul: so, when something is *willed*, a metabolic process happens, which is the

* In German, *Vorstellen*. Please recall that this means "a placing before oneself inwardly," not necessarily as a visual image. Ed.

bodily foundation for what is experienced in the soul as willing.

Now, in the soul a fully conscious, wakeful experience is present only with respect to the mental picturing mediated by our nervous system. What is mediated by the breathing rhythm lives in ordinary consciousness with about the same intensity as dream pictures. To this belongs everything of a feeling nature: all emotions, passions, and so on. Our willing, which is based on metabolic processes, is experienced in a degree of consciousness no higher than that present in the completely dim consciousness of our sleeping state. A more detailed study of the pertinent facts will show that we experience our willing in a completely different way than our mental picturing. We experience the latter the way one sees a colored surface, as it were; we experience willing as a kind of black area upon a colored field. We see something within the area where no color is, in fact, because, in contrast with its surroundings from which color impressions go forth, no such impressions come to meet us: We can picture willing mentally because, within the soul's experiences of mental pictures, at certain places, a nonpicturing inserts itself that places itself into our fully conscious experience the same way, in sleep, interruptions of consciousness place themselves into the conscious course of life. The manifoldness in our soul experience—in mental picturing, feeling, and willing—results from these different kinds of conscious experience.

In his book *Guidelines of Physiological Psychology*, Theodor Ziehen is led to significant characterizations of feeling and willing. In many ways, this book is a prime example of today's natural-scientific way of regarding the connection between the physical and the psychic elements in man.

134

Mental picturing, in all its different forms, is brought into the same connection with the nervous system that the anthroposophical viewpoint also must recognize. About feeling, however, Ziehen says:

> Almost without exception, earlier psychology regarded the emotions as the manifestations of a particular independent soul capacity. Kant placed the feeling of pleasure and pain, as a particular soul faculty, between the capacity for knowledge and the capacity for desire, and emphasized explicitly that any further tracing of these three soul capacities back to a common ground was not possible. In contrast to this view, our previous discussions have already shown that feelings of pleasure and pain do not exist at all in this kind of independence, but rather arise only as characteristics or traits—as the so-called nuances of feeling—of sensations and mental pictures.

So this way of thinking ascribes to feeling no independence in our soul life; it sees in feeling only a trait of mental picturing. The result is that it regards not only our life in mental picturing but also our feeling life as being founded upon nerve processes. For it, the nervous system is that part of the body to which the whole soul element is assigned. But this way of thinking, after all, is based on the fact that unconsciously it has already thought up in advance what it wants its findings to be. It grants the status of "soul element" only to what is related to nerve processes, and therefore must regard what cannot be assigned to the nervous system—feeling—as having no independent existence, as being a mere attribute of mental picturing. Anyone who does not set off in the wrong direction with his concepts in this manner and is *unbiased* in his soul observations will recognize the independence of our feeling life in the most definite way; and secondly, the unbiased evaluation of physiological knowledge will give the insight that feeling must be assigned to the breathing rhythm in the way described above.

The natural-scientific way of thinking denies to will any independent being within our soul life. Will does not even have the status—as feeling does—of being an attribute of mental picturing. But this denial is also based only on the fact that one wants to assign everything of a real soul nature to nerve processes. Now one cannot, however, relate willing in its own particular nature to actual nerve processes. Precisely when one works this through with exemplary clarity as Theodore Ziehen does, can one be impelled to the view that the analysis of soul processes in their relation to the life of the body "offers no cause to assume any separate will capacity." And yet: unbiased observation of the soul compels one to recognize an independent life of will; and a realistic insight into physiological findings shows that willing as such must not be brought into relation to nerve processes but rather to metabolic processes.

If one wishes to create clear concepts in this realm, one must view physiological and psychological findings in the light demanded by reality; but not in the way this occurs in today's physiology and psychology, where light is shed from preconceptions, definitions, and even in fact from theoretical sympathies and antipathies. Above all, we must take a hard look at the interrelations of nerve activity, breathing rhythm, and metabolic activity. For, these forms of activity do not lie *side by side*; they lie *in* one another; they interpenetrate; they go over into each other. Metabolic activity is present in the entire organism; it permeates the organs of rhythm and of nerve activity. But it is *not* the bodily foundation of feeling in rhythm; in nerve activity, it is *not* the basis of mental picturing; rather in both of them, the working will that permeates rhythm and nerves is to be assigned to the metabolic activity. Only a materialistic bias can make a connection between what exists in the nerve as metabolic activity and mental picturing. A study rooted in reality says something completely different. It must recognize that metabolism is present in the nerve insofar as will permeates it. Likewise, metabolism is present in the bodily apparatus of rhythm. The metabolic activity in this apparatus has to do with the will present in this organ. One must connect willing with metabolic activity and feeling with rhythmical occurrences, no matter which organ it is in which metabolism or rhythm appears. In the nerves, however, something completely different from metabolism and rhythm is occurring. The bodily processes in the nervous system that provide the basis of mental picturing are difficult to grasp physiologically. For, where nerve activity occurs, there the mental picturing of ordinary consciousness is present. The reverse is also true, however: where mental picturing is not being done, there no nerve activity is ever to be found, but only metabolic activity in the nerve and a nuance of rhythmical function. Physiology will never arrive at concepts that are in accordance with reality in the study of the nerves as long as it does not understand that true nerve activity absolutely cannot be an object of physiological sense observation. Anatomy and physiology must arrive at the knowledge that they can discover nerve activity only through a *method of exclusion*. What is *not* sense-perceptible in the life of the nerve, but whose presence—and even its

137

characteristic way of working—is proved necessary by what is sense-perceptible: that is nerve activity. One arrives at a positive picture of nerve activity if one looks into that material happening by which the purely soul-spiritual being of a living content of our mental picturing—as described in the first essay of this book—is lamed down into the lifeless mental picturing of ordinary consciousness. Without this concept, which one must introduce into physiology, there is no possibility in that science of stating what nerve activity is. Physiology has developed methods for itself that at present conceal rather than reveal this concept. And even psychology has blocked its own path in this region. Just look, for example, at how Herbartian psychology has worked in this direction. It has turned its gaze only upon the life of our mental picturing, and sees in feeling and willing only effects of our life in mental picturing. But these effects melt away before the approach of knowledge, if at the same time one does not direct one's gaze in an unbiased way upon the reality of feeling and willing. Through such melting away one cannot arrive at any realistic coordinating of feeling and willing with bodily processes.

The *body as a whole*, not merely the nerve activity included in it, is the physical basis of our soul life. And just as for ordinary consciousness our soul life can be transcribed as mental picturing, feeling, and willing, so can our bodily life as nerve activity, rhythmical function, and metabolic processes.

Immediately the question arises: How does our actual sense perception—which is only an extension of nerve activity—integrate itself into the organism, on the one hand; and on the other hand, how does our ability to move—to which willing leads—integrate itself? Unbiased observation shows that neither belong to the organism in the same sense as nerve activity, rhythmical function, and metabolic processes. What occurs in a sense organ is something that does not belong directly to the organism at all. With our senses we have the outer world stretching like gulfs into the being of the organism. While the soul is encompassing in a sense organ an outer happening, the soul is not taking part in an inner organic happening, but rather in the continuation of the outer happening into the organism. (I mentioned these inner connections epistemologically in a lecture to the Bologna Philosophy Conference in 1911.[*])

In a process of movement we also do not have to do physically with something whose essential being lies inside the organism, but rather with a working of the organism in relationships of balance and forces in which the organism is placed with respect to the outer world. Within the organism, the will is only assigned the role of a metabolic process; but the happening caused by this process is at the same time an actuality within the outer world's interrelation of balance and forces; and by being active in willing, the soul transcends the realm of the organism and participates with its deeds in the happenings of the outer world.

The division of nerves into sensory and motor nerves has created terrible confusion in the study of all these things. No matter how deeply rooted this division may seem to be in today's physiological picture of things, it is not based on unbiased observation. What physiology presents on the basis of nerve severance or of pathological elimination of certain nerves does *not* prove what appears upon the foundation of experiment or outer experience; it proves

---

[*] Published as *Seeing with the Soul*, Mercury Press, 1996.

139

something completely different. It proves that the difference is not there at all which one assumes to exist between sensory and motor nerves. On the contrary, both kinds of nerves are of the *same nature*. The so-called motor nerve does *not* serve movement in the sense assumed in the teachings of the division theory; rather, as *the bearer of nerve activity* it serves the inner perception of that metabolic process that underlies our willing, in just the same way as the sensory nerve serves the perception of what takes place in the sense organ. Until the study of the nerves works with clear concepts in this regard, a correct relation of our soul life to the life of the body will not come about.

* * *

In the same way that psycho-physiologically one can seek the relation to the body's life of the soul life that runs its course in mental picturing, feeling, and willing, so one can also strive anthroposophically for knowledge of the relation which the soul element of ordinary consciousness has to spiritual life. And there one discovers through the anthroposophical methods described in this and in my other books, that just as our mental picturing finds a bodily foundation in our nerve activity, so it also finds a basis in the spiritual realm. In the other direction—on the side turned away from the body—the soul stands in a relation to a spiritually real element that is the foundation for the mental picturing of ordinary consciousness. This spiritual element, however, can only be experienced by a seeing cognition. And it is experienced through its content being presented to seeing consciousness as differentiated Imaginations. Just as, toward the body, our mental picturing is based on nerve activity, so

140

from the other side, it streams toward us out of a spiritually real element, revealing itself in Imaginations. This spiritually real element is what is called in my books the etheric or life body. (In speaking about the etheric body I always emphasize expressly that one should take exception neither to the word "body" nor to the word "etheric"; for, what I present shows clearly that one should not interpret the matter in a materialistic sense.) And this life body (in the fourth volume of the first year of the periodical, *"Das Reich,"* I also used the expression "body of formative forces") is the spiritual element from which our ordinary consciousness' life of mental picturing flows from birth (or conception, as it were) until death.

The feeling in our ordinary consciousness is based, on the bodily side, upon the rhythmical function. From the spiritual side it flows from a spiritually real element that is discovered in anthroposophical research by methods that I call "Inspiration" in my writings. (Again, it should be noted that by this concept I mean only what I have paraphrased in my work; so one should not confuse this term with what lay people understand by this word.) To the seeing consciousness the spiritually real being underlying the soul and attainable to Inspiration is his own spiritual being, transcending birth and death. This is the region where anthroposophy undertakes its spiritual-scientific investigations into the question of human immortality. *Just as in the body, through the rhythmic function, the mortal part of man's feeling nature manifests itself, so, in the content of Inspiration of seeing consciousness, does the immortal spiritual core of our soul being manifest.*

For seeing consciousness, our willing, which toward the body is based on metabolic processes, streams from the spirit through what in my writings I call "Intuition." What manifests in the body through the—in a certain way—lowest activity of the metabolism corresponds in the spirit to the highest: what expresses itself through Intuitions. Therefore, mental picturing, which is based on nerve activity, comes almost to full expression in the body; willing shows only a weak reflection in the metabolic processes oriented toward it in the body. Our real mental picturing is the *living one*; the mental picturing determined by the body is the lamed one. The content is the same. Real willing, even that which realizes itself in the physical world, runs its course in regions accessible only to Intuitive vision; its bodily counterpart has almost nothing to do with this content. Within that spiritually real being that manifests itself to Intuition is contained what extends over from previous earth lives into the following ones. And it is in the realm that comes into consideration here that anthroposophy approaches the questions of repeated earth lives and of destiny.

As the body lives itself out in nerve activity, rhythmical function, and metabolic processes, so the spirit of man lives in what manifests itself in Imaginations, Inspirations, and Intuitions. And as in its realm the body allows for an experience of the nature of *its* outer world in two directions—in sensory processes, namely, and in processes of movement—so the spirit also: in one direction through the fact that it experiences *Imaginatively* our mentally picturing soul life, even in ordinary consciousness, and in the other direction through the fact that in willing it unfolds *Intuitive* impulses that realize themselves in metabolic processes. If one looks toward the body, one finds the nerve activity that lives as the element of mental picturing; if one looks toward the spirit, one becomes aware of the spirit content of Imaginations that flows into this very element of mental picturing. Brentano feels at first the spiritual side of the mental picturing life of the soul; he therefore characterizes this life as a picture life (an imaginative happening). When not merely one's own inner soul life is experienced, however, but also—through *judgment*—an element of acceptance or rejection, then there is added to our mental picturing a soul experience, flowing from the spirit, whose content remains unconscious as long as we are dealing only with ordinary consciousness, because this content consists of Imaginations of a spiritually real element that underlies the physical object and that only adds to the mental picture *the fact that its content exists.*

It is for this reason that in his classification Brentano splits our life of mental pictures into *mere mental picturing*, which only experiences imaginatively an inwardly existing element, and into *judging*, which experiences imaginatively something given from without, but which brings the experience to consciousness only as an acceptance or rejection. With respect to *feeling*, Brentano does not look at all at its bodily foundation, the rhythmical function; he only brings into the realm of his attention what arises from Inspirations (that remain unconscious) as loving and hating within the region of ordinary consciousness. *Willing* escapes his attention completely, however, because his attention wishes to direct itself only upon phenomena *in the soul*, whereas in willing there lies something that is *not* enclosed within the soul, something through which the soul experiences also an outer world. Brentano's classification of soul phenomena, therefore, is based on the fact that he divides them according to viewpoints that can be seen in their true light only when one turns one's gaze upon the spiritual core of the soul, and on the fact that he wants to apply his classification only to the phenomena of ordinary consciousness. With what is said here about Brentano I only wished to supplement what was said on this subject on page 74ff.

Addendum 7 to pages 69 and 80:
Brentano's Separation of the Soul Element from What Is External to the Soul.

Through his different presentations Brentano shows how strongly he strove for a clear separating of the soul element from what is external to the soul. His concept of the soul, which we have described in this book, compels him to do this. In order to see this, let us look at the way he tries to define the soul experience we have in forming a conviction about a truth. He asks himself: What is the source of what the soul experiences as a conviction when it relates this conviction to a content of mental pictures? Some thinkers believe that, with respect to a given truth, the degree of conviction is determined by the intensity of feeling with which one experiences the corresponding content of mental pictures. Brentano says about this:

> It is wrong—but it is an error embraced by almost everyone, and one from which I also had not yet freed myself when I wrote the first volume of my *Psychology*—to believe that the degree of conviction is a level of intensity in judging that could be analogous to the intensity of pleasure and pain. If Windelband had reproached me with *this* error, I would consider him to be completely right. But now he criticizes me for wanting to accept intensity only in an analogous sense (not in the same sense) in the case of a conviction, and for declaring that in terms of magnitude one cannot compare the supposed intensity of conviction with the actual intensity of feeling. There we have the results of his improved grasp of what a judgment is.

145

If the degree of conviction in my belief that 2+1=3 *were* an intensity, how powerful this intensity would have to be! And if now, as Windelband would have it, this belief were made into a feeling— not just something that could be thought of as analogous to a feeling—how destructive for our nervous system the vehemence of a stirred feeling would be! Every doctor would have to warn against the study of mathematics as something shattering to one's health.

If Brentano could have lived more deeply into what worked in him in his striving to discover the nature of conviction, he would have seen the separation that exists between the mentally picturing soul element—which does not experience *any* intensity within itself when a conviction is being formed—and what is external to the soul—which enters the content of the soul element and which in the intensity of the degree of conviction, also remains something external to the soul while *in* the soul, in such a way that our inner life does indeed *observe* the degree of conviction, but does not live in it.

What Brentano presents in his essay "The Individuation, Multiple Quality, and Intensity of Sense-perceptible Phenomena" (in his book *Investigations into a Psychology of the Senses*) belongs in a similar sphere of strict separation between the soul element and what is external to the soul. He endeavors to show there that intensity is not inherent to the actual soul element, and that the degree of intensity of soul sensation represents a life of what is felt outside the soul and is now present upon the stage of the soul element. Brentano senses that one absolutely does not need to enter into the "mystical darkness" of nonscience when one is endeavoring to develop further in cognition the seeds planted in such elementary insights. Therefore, he writes at the end of the essay just mentioned:

It is easy to see what the wider significance of this is.

Look how much *Herbart's psychology* and also *psychophysics* were founded upon this dogma (he is referring to the dogma of the intensity of the soul element)! All that will be torn down also in its fall. And so we'll see how the correction of a small point in the science of soul sensation will exert a far-reaching reformatory influence.

Even the *hypotheses that one has set up relative to the world-all* will not remain untouched by it.

To a large extent one has declared that a common analogy prevails between the psychic and the physical realms, without any proof being offered, to be sure, or even seriously attempted. One kept entirely to generalities and so an assigned role sufficed for the thought of intensity as a kind of magnitude belonging to every soul entity just as a spatial magnitude belongs to every physical entity.

But if one declares a common analogy to prevail between the soul element and the physical element, why not go all the way and declare them to be identical or simply substitute one for the other?

In everything analogous to the physical and vouched for in itself only through the evidence of perception, the soul element must render superfluous any hypothetical assumption that anything physical exists.

So, among others, Wundt's psychology also ends up with the thought that, after heuristically attributing an existence to the physical world for a time, one could finally let this assumption of physical existence fall away like scaffolding, in which case the whole genuine truth would reveal itself as a purely psychic world edifice.

This thought, to be sure, until now has had little prospect of ever gaining tangible form or being elaborated in detail. Any hopes in this direction, however, have been completely dashed by the new concept of intensity with its clear proof that nothing could be farther from the truth than calling the magnitude of intensity a universal property of soul activities.

So we will never allow our belief in the true existence of a physical world to be taken away from us, and this belief will always remain for natural science the *hypothesis of hypotheses.*

The common analogy between the soul element and the physical element, which Brentano rejects, is only sought by someone who does not strive to picture clearly the soul element on the one hand and *the* physical element on the other, but rather, instead of this—while continuing with his concepts to feel his way along against the physical—attributes to the soul element experiences like that of intensity, whereas, in the purely soul element, nothing of it is to be found. It seems to me that the above thought of Brentano's would have come more clearly into view, if its bearer—in the sense of what was described in this book on page 69f.— had focused his attention upon that characteristic of the

148

physical element which is equal in significance to the intentional element within the soul element.

Nevertheless, it is significant that Brentano dared to extend his view beyond elementary insights out into more far-reaching, cosmic riddles. For, today's way of thinking is disinclined to broaden its views. Here is one example from many. At one place in his *Eight Psychological Lectures* (Jena, 1869), the eminent psychologist Fortlage shows how close he was with his cognitive inklings to a certain region of seeing consciousness, to the region, namely, of knowledge of the laming power of the soul existence living in our ordinary consciousness. On page 35 he writes:

> When we call ourselves "living beings," and thus ascribe to ourselves a characteristic that we share with animals and plants, we necessarily understand the "living state" to mean something that never leaves us, and continues on in us in sleep and in the waking state. This is the vegetative life of the nutrition of our organism, an unconscious life, a life of sleep. The brain is an exception to this through the fact that this nutritive life, this sleeping life, is outweighed in the brain during the pauses of wakefulness by a consuming life (what I have called "laming down" in this book). During these pauses the brain is given over predominantly to being consumed, and consequently falls into a state that, if extended to the other organs, would bring about the absolute debilitation of the body or death.

And taking this thought to its conclusion, Fortlage says (page 39): "Consciousness is a little, a partial death; death is a large and total consciousness, an *awakening of the whole being in its innermost depths*." One can only say that Fortlage stands with his thoughts at the starting point of anthroposophy, even though, like Brentano, he does not enter. Nevertheless, even because of his standing at the starting point, Eduard von Hartmann, who is completely under the spell of today's way of picturing things, finds that a perspective extending out beyond elementary knowledge into the great cosmic riddle of human immortality is scientifically untenable. Eduard von Hartmann writes of Fortlage: "He steps outside the boundaries of psychology when he describes consciousness as a little and partial death, and death as a large and total consciousness, as a clearer, total awakening of the soul in all its depths...." (Please see Eduard von Hartmann, *Modern Psychology*, Leipzig, 1901)

Addendum 8 to page 90:
An Objection Often Raised against Anthroposophy

An objection is often raised against anthroposophy that is just as comprehensible to the soul attitude of the personality from which it comes as it is unjustified to the spirit from which anthroposophical research is undertaken. This objection seems to me to be entirely insignificant because its refutation is near at hand for anyone who follows with true understanding the presentations made from the anthroposophical point of view. Only because it arises ever anew do I say something about it here, as I have already done also in the sixth edition of *Theosophy*, 1914, at the end.

In order to raise this objection, the demand is made that the results of spiritual observation which anthroposophy is presenting be "proven" in the sense of purely natural-scientific methods of experimentation. One imagines, for example, that several people who assert that they can arrive at such results are confronted by a number of other people in a properly ordered experiment, and the "spiritual researchers" would then say what they have "seen" about the subjects in front of them. Their statements would then have to agree, or at least be similar in a sufficiently high percentage. It is comprehensible that someone who only knows anthroposophy without having understood it will raise this demand again and again, for its fulfillment would spare him the trouble of working his own way through to the correct path of proof which consists in the attainment of one's *own* vision, which is possible for everyone. Anyone who has really understood anthroposophy, however, also sees that an experiment set up in the way just described to gain the results of truly spiritual vision is about as appropriate as stopping the hands on a clock in order to tell time. For, in order to bring about the conditions under which something spiritual can be seen, paths must be taken that arise from circumstances of the soul life itself. Outer arrangements like those leading to a natural-scientific experiment are not formed out of such soul circumstances. These circumstances must be such, for example, that the will impulse leading to vision issue *exclusively* and *entirely* from the primal, individual, inner impulse of the person who is to see. And that there is nothing in the way of artificial outer measures flowing into and shaping this inner impulse.

It is actually surprising that the fact is so little considered that everyone, after all, through one's own appropriate soul attitude, can directly create for oneself the proofs for the truth of anthroposophy; that therefore these "proofs" are accessible to everyone. As little as one wants to admit this to oneself, the fact is that the reasons for requiring "outer proofs" lie, after all, only in the fact that outer proofs would be attainable in a more comfortable way than upon the difficult, uncomfortable, but truly spiritual-scientific path.

What Brentano wanted, when he endeavored again and again to be able to work in a psychological laboratory, lies in an entirely different direction than this demand for comfortable experimental proofs for anthroposophical truths. His longing to have such a laboratory at his disposal often appears in his writings. The circumstances denying him this affected his life tragically. Precisely through his approach to psychological questions he would have accomplished great things with such a laboratory. If one wishes, in fact, to establish the *best* foundation for anthropological-psychological findings, extending to the "borderland of knowledge" where anthropology and anthroposophy must meet, this can best be accomplished through a psychological laboratory such as Brentano envisaged. In order to demonstrate the facts of a "seeing consciousness" no experimental methods would need to be sought in such a laboratory; but through *those* experimental methods that are sought, it would become clear how the being of man is predisposed to this vision, and how seeing consciousness is demanded by ordinary consciousness. Anyone who stands upon the anthroposophical viewpoint longs as Brentano did to be able to work in a genuine psychological laboratory—which is impossible because of the prejudices still holding sway today against anthroposophy.

Addendum 9
Closing Remark

I shall not go into all the "attacks" that have been made recently, not against anthroposophy, but against me personally. This is not appropriate here partly because these attacks lack any true scientific character; and for the other part, they are of a purely personal nature, are not based on any factual foundation but upon hatefulness, and in the great majority of cases the attackers know quite well that their assertions are objective untruths.

Appendix:
Dessoir's Response to Steiner's Essay on Him

Those who have worked their way through this essay might be interested in studying an extended passage of Max Dessoir's writing. The first quotation is the opening paragraph of his preface to the first edition of *Beyond the Soul* (*Vom Jenseits der Seele*), 1917. It is indicative of the "scientific" and human level of the whole book:

> For a long time now, German science has exercised the most extreme restraint with respect to the field that we are to deal with here. And not without good reason. Serious, life-filling research tends to be conservative in its approach, especially when conducted within a working community—as in universities—whereas the amateur science [*Liebhaberwissenschaft*] of isolated individuals throws itself light-heartedly into the arms of what is new or striking. The scientific sense for cleanliness avoids contact with that murky circle in which charlatans and falsifiers, half-crazy females, and pretentious scatterbrains do their thing. It seems to us beneath our dignity, repugnant, time-consuming, and useless to bother ourselves at all about the mischief of spiritists and faith-healers, the fantasies of the theosophists, and the silly hair-splitting of modern cabalists.

The following quotation is from the preface of the second edition of Max Dessoir's *Beyond the Soul*, 1920. It is his response to Rudolf Steiner's essay and provides a classic study of the tactics necessary to someone who is careless about the truth:

> ...In the chapter on anthroposophy, to be sure, I have made no changes, because Herr Dr. Steiner, in his recently published book *Riddles of the Soul*, zeros in on my word choice; so everything better remain as it was. With the second part of the Steinerian book the fact of the matter is

namely: Steiner escapes from any factual discussion by asserting that what I presented has nothing at all to do with his views, that I read his books incompletely and superficially, and that my version of his work was almost entirely a distortion and falsification. In order to show this, for seventy pages he conducts "a little bit of philology." Oh, if only it were good philology! But it is all pettifoggery, hair-splitting, and much worse, intended to divert attention from the main points. Mr. Steiner says that he regrets being forced to do what he does, and I am happy to believe that he did not feel so well as he was doing it. I am absolutely unable to express how heavily it weighs upon me to enter into this kind of conflict. For, the only real point at issue, little is gained; Steiner's adherents will probably hear little about my refutation, or if they do, will remain true to their master's watchword; what is more, I am at a disadvantage since I do not have seventy pages at my disposal. Nevertheless I would like to respond, in order to spare the friends of my book any doubts they may have.

Let us begin with the first page that is dealt with in more detail, page 254. Here my assailant nails a word that seems suitable to him for proving the low degree of my scientific exactitude. There I call *The Philosophy of Spiritual Activity* Steiner's "first" work (*Erstling*). "The truth is that my literary activity begins with my introductions to Goethe's natural-scientific works." Sure. It is only that, with a really amazing coolness, Steiner is silent on the fact that I communicate this same "truth" on the third and fourth lines of my book, to the effect, namely, that I am speaking of a "first" work relative to theosophy—as the context in which this word appears also shows clearly.

To the factual statements about that book is added then: "Look and see whether there is anything in *The Philosophy of Spiritual Activity* that could be synthesized into such monstrously trivial statements." I looked it up and found the following:

Steiner: "We have, it is true, torn ourselves away from nature; but we must nevertheless have taken something over with us into our own being....We can find nature outside us only when we first know it within us. What is akin to it in our own inner being will be our guide. Thus our course is sketched out for us." [end of chapter 2.] and further: There is a reason why we can know thinking "more directly and more intimately than any other process of the world. Just because we bring it forth ourselves, we know the characteristics of its course....What is impossible with respect to nature, namely, creating before knowing, we do accomplish with respect to thinking." [Chapter 3.]

My (Dessoir's) paraphrase:

In Steiner's *The Philosophy of Spiritual Activity* it is stated "that man has taken over into himself something from nature, and therefore, through knowledge of his own being, can solve the riddle of nature; that, in thinking, a creative activity precedes knowing, whereas we are not involved in the coming about of nature and so are dependent on knowing it subsequently."

Does that suffice? In the last sentence, left out here,*of my quote from my footnote on page 254—which, as an almost verbatim paraphrase, Steiner cannot easily deny—Steiner censures the little word "merely," even though it only means that his teachings on intuition in that first theosophical work have not yet been fully unfolded. Furthermore, with very evil fallout, he turns against my sentence on page 255: "When our soul powers are enhanced,...the 'I,' in its perception of colors and sounds, can even exclude the mediation of the body from this experience." The basis for this—not the whole basis, to be sure—was a passage in the book *Riddles of Philosophy*, whose "nonuse" is held up to me by Steiner. There one can read: "And a true knowledge of our ordinary soul life does present itself as one of our first experiences when this new spiritual life has been attained. In reality, even our ordinary soul life is not produced by the body, but rather runs its course outside the body. When I see a color, when I hear a sound, I do not experience the color or sound as resulting from my body; rather, as a self-con-

---

* Why?! Please see page 47f. of this book! Ed.

scious 'I,' I am connected outside of my body with the color or sound. The task of the body is to function as a kind of mirror....The human body is not a producer of perceptions, nor of any soul life; it is an apparatus for reflecting what takes place in a soul-spiritual way outside of the body."

On that same page 255 I called the cross a symbol for "annihilated lower drives," whereas Steiner called it a symbol for the "annihilated lower element of our drives." Steiner takes this deviation—which, please note, does not occur in a direct quotation or anything—as cause for highly excited reproaches and ends with the statement: "Only with respect to these misrepresentations is Dessoir's critique possible." That is pretty strong medicine, for—I did not mount any critique at all on this point! Bewildered by this, one must ask oneself: Can blindness really go this far?

On page 257 Steiner discovers another example of that superficial and distorted reportage for which he chastises me in front of the "1 through 4,000" readers of his first edition. He, Steiner, is not explaining the objective fact of a limb's so-called "going to sleep" as resulting from the separation of the etheric body. "Only if one takes my formulations the way they are given can one form an opinion as to the significance of my statements..." We had best keep quiet about the significance of the statement, but how do matters stand relative to the formulation? Here it is: "During our life between birth and death a separation of the etheric body occurs only as an exception and only for a short while. For example, if someone puts pressure on a limb, a part of his etheric body can separate from the physical. We say of a limb where this has occurred that it has "gone to sleep." And the strange sensation that one feels then results from the separation of the etheric body. (Of course, a materialistic way of picturing things can also deny here the invisible element present in the visible, and state that this all results only from the physical disturbance caused by the pressure.) In a case like this, clairvoyant observation can see how the corresponding part of the etheric body extends out from the physical." (*Occult Science, an Outline*) I really do not know how it could be an objective blunder, and possibly even a moral failing, for me to have been so bold as to assert that we others "do not wish, with Steiner, to 'explain' the 'going to sleep' of a leg through the separation of the etheric body from the physical body."

After all this, I am almost happy to admit that Steiner, in an objection to page 258 of my book, is correct to some extent. I say there that "through" the spiritual beings assumed by Steiner processes of nutrition and excretion supposedly "developed" on Saturn, whereas I should have expressed myself as Steiner demands, more exactly—and also more in detail, to be sure, than is possible in a brief summary—to the effect that through an "interaction" in the etheric body of that entity "an activity arises that now in its turn leads to the nutritional and excretory processes of the primal planetary form." I emphatically request the reader to extend my sentence accordingly, and furthermore I beg him most urgently to take note of the fact that he does not after all live in the sixth "Post-Atlantean cultural epoch," but in the fifth. For my part, however, he can believe that I am not particularly upset about my mistaken number, because for me these Post-Atlantean periods *and* those nutritional processes in the primal planetary form are just humbug.

I now come to page 260. The focal point is the passage "Especially a person who himself teaches wisdom..." Steiner wishes to show what "Dessoir does by retailoring the relevant passage of my book for his readers." The "relevant" German is pitiful and its coarseness certainly obvious (curious, in what tones anthroposophical refinement lets itself be heard). Nevertheless we must linger here for a moment. Before the sentence that I quoted verbatim, there was, among other things, the following: a person who is joined by adherents, "through genuine self-knowledge, can easily become aware that precisely the fact that he has found adherents gives him the feeling that what he has to say does not originate from him." Several general thoughts follow, among them the ones I cite, and then Steiner continues: "Socrates experienced something like this....Many efforts have been made to explain this 'daimon' of Socrates. But one can explain it only if one wishes to give oneself over to the thought that Socrates was able to feel something like what is described in the above discussion." These presentations are supposedly reinterpreted in a malicious way in my book. Let us listen to Mr. Steiner: "Where I speak of Socrates, he twists the matter to seem that I am speaking about myself by stating, 'as Mr. Rudolf Steiner confesses' and even putting my name in italics. What are we dealing with here? With nothing less, in fact, than an *objective untruth*. I leave it up to any fair thinker to form a judgment about a critic who employs such means." Easy does it, Herr Dr. Steiner! Is it merely Socrates who is supposed to have experienced "something like" what is described in the "above" discussion, and is the "above" description a "genuine self-knowledge"? Are you perhaps denying that what is expressed here as a general case and later applied to Socrates stems from your own experience? Or do you yourself have no connection with the "spiritual powers from higher worlds"; does everything you recount to your gullible anthroposophists spring from your "ordinary consciousness"? And one more thing, Herr Dr. Steiner: do you really believe that my italicizing of your name is wicked of me? A man like yourself, who has published several thousand pages in your life, must have noticed that in my book, every time a writer's name appears on a page for the first time it is italicized.

Let that be enough. It fills me with burning shame that I could not simply remain silent about accusations that basically touch upon human integrity. As I wrote the pathological history of idealism in the last chapters of my book, I had no inkling that the historian would again be compelled to act as doctor. My personal experiences were more of a sort to make me tired and sad. I had learned to know occult researchers whose weakness in thinking was regarded as a power of inner enlightenment; I had to experience that valuable people are enticed by the empty will-o-the-wisp of spiritism or of faith-healing. Nevertheless, my aim was to take hold of all this with a cautious hand. The most important point, it seemed to me, would be to show that such strange contemporaries are not breathing in the morning air, but rather are surrounded by the thick fumes of the most ancient past. If this effort succeeds, then perhaps the living forces, hidden even here, of the purer forms of idealism could be won, just as from the phenomenological realm something can be rescued for science. Have I been too optimistic? I believe not. For ultimately:

Every flame is upward striving,
Every spirit kindles others,
Through the smoke of words is climbing
Mankind into azure silence.

Berlin, January 1918   M.D.

www.ingramcontent.com/pod-product-compliance
Lightning Source LLC
Chambersburg PA
CBHW032101080426

42733CB00006B/366